Jim Thom
Atlanta
Late summer, 2017

MW00711948

A New Gilded Age:

Stories and Essays

by

James M. Thomas

DORRANCE
PUBLISHING CO
EST. 1920
PITTSBURGH, PENNSYLVANIA 15238

Dorrance Publishing Co
585 Alpha Drive
Suite 103
Pittsburgh, PA 15238
Visit our website at *www.dorrancebookstore.com*

ISBN: 978-1-4809-3836-6
eISBN: 978-1-4809-3859-5

Other Books by James M. Thomas

Individual Integrity
Integrity: The Indispensable Element
Persuasive Speech
The Georgia We Want (Monograph)

Contents

Short Stories

Irwin Auker

Over half-a-century has passed, and my memory isn't what it once was. At best it was never above average. But I explicitly remember Irwin Auker's sojourn. Some of it I couldn't forget if I tried. And believe me; I have tried. So I shall begin where it began: on a clear September morning during "coffee hour," as we called it, in my hometown of Hudson, a farm town and county seat of Hurley County, Georgia. The year was 1962. That was when he appeared among us, unknown and unannounced. Twelve months later, he vanished. A lot happened while he was with us, and soon thereafter—a lot that left its mark on me.

Coffee hour was a simple, continuing custom in the everyday life of Hudson, population 3,500, in the fading heyday of small town America. The forum was Hal's Shell Station, a square, white-washed, concrete-block edifice with gas pumps out front. It had a Shell sign hanging overhead, standing hard by the intersection of State

Routes 26 and 36, Hudson's main thoroughfares—conspicuous as a fortress.

Proprietor Hal Dreyer began his workday at five o'clock in the morning. Following an unvarying routine, wearing tan coveralls with a yellow Shell emblem stitched on the back, the heavy-set, serious-minded Dreyer walked to work from his modest bungalow, two blocks north of the station. There he propped open its double-front doors, turned on the lights and the gas pumps, poured grounds from a can of Maxwell House into a two-gallon blue-speckled coffee pot, and set it on a gas burner, standing on iron legs adjacent to the red Coke machine. Hal's and the coffee hour were then ready for business.

And they came, drifting in and out while the world awakened. Some poured a quick cup and left. Others tarried and milled about. Meanwhile, as the morning sun rose through the Georgia pines and until it was time to go to work, the regulars merged, talked, and conversed. We sat on a wooden bench, in a few nondescript chairs, or atop empty soft-drink crates turned on end, in a haphazard semi-circle, facing the Coke machine and watching through the station's store front windows as the town came to life. Surrounding us from floor to ceiling, suspended, shelved, and crated was Hal's inventory: car tires, inner tubes, crated engines, fan belts, grease cans, cartons of motor oil, tools and tool boxes, assorted auto parts, and brand new windshields. We came for coffee, the warmth of friends, the latest news, gossip, weather reports, poli-

tics, opinions, jokes, stories, a good laugh. All flowed free
and unfettered.

At the time, I was two years out of ag school with a degree in agronomy and busy as hell on Dad Stoddard's big
farm, all 850 acres of it that lay due west of Hudson's city
limits. About tillage and tilth, soil chemistry, hybrid seeds,
and field crops, I knew a lot. Otherwise I was green and
inexperienced. My understandings of man and society
were shallow indeed. I'm talking about real living in the
real word: the realm of fate and circumstance, success and
failure, disappointment and triumph, happiness and despair, sickness and death; the realm of seen and unseen ties
that bind friends, townsmen, counties, and communities.
To my credit, however, I was responsive and a good lis-
tener and coffee hour for me was a natural, a joy. Dad's
grumbling aside, I rarely missed.

Somewhere I have a grainy black and white photo-
graph of Hal's duly assembled coffee hour regulars, taken
by somebody from the Hudson *Times*. There I sit of a
morning, a grinning speaking likeness—young, optimistic,
and largely unaware. How strange it is to look at now, a
mere image that evokes both pleasure and pain. Also, it
returns me to the starting point.

For I was among the six or eight still in place the
morning Auker walked in. While our chatter rose and fell,
he stepped through the open doors—a man of dark complexion, average height, gaunt, and clearly underweight.
He was wearing loosely fitting khakis, a blue plaid shirt,

his thick brown hair barbered in a brush cut. I guessed he was in his mid-forties, an accurate guess as it turned out.

With movements smooth and easy, he circled our small enclave like he was evading smoke from a woods fire. Seeing no opening, he paused at the edge and stood stock still. Drawing my attention was his rugged, square-jawed face—that unforgettable face—the face that from time to time still pierces my dreams. It was clamped tight as a death mask. Red-haired Alvin Arnold, my gregarious, life-long pal and best friend, then the State Farm Agent for Hurley County, spotted Auker and spoke up. "Grab yourself a crate over there, fella, and join us," he said, pointing to a stack of empty Coke crates against the big room's west wall. Auker complied, and I got a closer look. The bags beneath his eyes were puffy. When lighting a Pall Mall, he held the Zippo with both hands. They trembled visibly.

Without comment, though clearly attentive, he remained in place that morning until we adjourned, then rose and walked out with neither a nod nor a word. I watched as he drove away in a battered blue Ford station wagon.

"Who's the newcomer?" I asked Alvin and our mutual friend, attorney J. R. Jones, as we sauntered outside, knowing that if anyone knew Jones would. A respected lawyer and state representative, the white-haired, perceptive Jones, whose face and thickening waist were showing the wear of the years, placed priority on keeping up with events, personal and impersonal, in Hurley County and beyond.

"His name's Auker," said Jones, slowly and deliberately. "I think he's Nevaada Miller's nephew. I have it he's staying with her in the big house over on Third Street... up from Miami they say. Nobody knows for sure why he's here."

That exhausted J. R.'s profile. Alvin had no leads at all. Hence we parted and went our separate ways that late summer morning, with skies over Hurley County growing as azure as those over Havana and autumn, always the best season of the year in farm country, lying just ahead.

When I arrived at Hal's two mornings later, Auker had entered again and was seated, silently sipping from a styrofoam cup. I drew one from the scalding pot, turned up a Coke crate, took a place beside him, and instinctively extended a hand. "I'm Jason Stoddard," I said.

"Irwin Auker," he replied, in crisp clipped tones, taking my hand and staring at me with eyes the color of coal—two orbs sunk deep in the hollows of a forlorn face. Instantly he turned back to the hour's verbal flow, but it was long enough. Even I, the untutored, perceived he was beset by a misery I neither knew nor understood.

For a time, he was rarely seen around Hudson save at coffee hour. There he became a fixture—observant, silent, withdrawn, seated always at the outer edge. From these daily appearances, I concluded Auker gained a sense of reassurance and reality, limited perhaps, but nonetheless a

7

balm of some kind to a distressed mind. Coming and going at Hal's, he and I began exchanging greetings.

Just as one with a broken leg must learn to walk again, Auker began a slow climb out of his shell. The evidence was plain to see the morning he followed me from the post office. He had put on pounds and looked healthier. His countenance was lighter and his step quicker. On the rugged features of his face, I saw for the first time the trace of a smile.

"Got a minute?" he asked.

"Absolutely," I answered, pleased to see him in better spirits.

"Thanks for the *coffee hour*, as y'all call it."

"Hell, we're glad to have you. It's an open forum, you know."

"I know, but I'm glad it's there... helps me start the day... something to look forward to... the guys... the palaver," he said, looking off and into the distance. "Sorry I haven't contributed to the commentary, so to speak."

"No rule says you have to," I said, and sensing he was about to break it off, pushed the dialogue and inquired, "You're from Miami?"

"Right."

"Mind telling me what brought you to Hudson?" speaking as politely as I knew how.

Looking around to see if others were in earshot, he said, "I don't mind. It will all come out sooner or later, I'm sure."

Detecting I may have struck something deep, I quickly added, "Look, Irwin, I don't mean to pry."

"No, it's all right," he continued. "I came up here to get out of the Miami madhouse and try and pull myself back together. The doctor suggested it... said I needed a quieter setting and time to stabilize...to recover my health...his words...among others," looking down and weakly kicking at loose pebbles.

I saw more was coming and waited.

"To tell you the truth, Jason, I'm up here trying to get over a goddamn breakdown," he said, through clenched teeth.

"I'm sorry," was all I could think of.

He went on. "Over the years, June and I kept in touch with Aunt Nevaada. When things fell apart, she offered her fine old home as an asylum. And there you have it," he said, turning and striding away.

He left a lot unsaid, I thought as I drove out to the farm that day. What was it that 'fell apart' in Florida? What would drive a guy like Auker to a 'breakdown' as he called it? Nevaada Miller supplied answers and filled in gaps.

"Miss Nevaada," as she was known in Hudson, was one if its distinguished citizens. A widow by ten years of Thornton Miller, owner and operator of the section's largest fertilizer plant, and one of its wealthiest business-men, she was then in her 70s but still active and alert. She was tall and thin, wore colorful long skirts and clear-framed spectacles and tied her grey hair in a tight bun. She determinedly drove a polished black Buick with never as much as a dent. She lived alone in the two-story white house with high gables, green shutters, and expansive lawns, served by the ever faithful Florence, her cook and housekeeper of four decades. I had known her and her late husband all my life. Growing up in Hudson, I delivered her newspapers, mowed her Bermuda grass lawns, and considered her the dearest of friends. She was also a walking repository of the town's history, its people, and its lore.

Walking out of church together one Sunday morning, she drew me aside to talk about Irwin. She informed me he was the only child of her brother, Malcolm, once a small farmer in Hurley County. When Irwin was in grade school, the family moved to South Florida where he grew up and graduated from high school. When World War II broke out, he was drafted and saw lots of heavy fighting in the Pacific. After the war, he settled in Miami, attended a technical school on the GI Bill, met and married June.

"She's one lovely woman…a devoted wife and mother…the love of his life. I don't think Irwin's ever looked at another woman," she said. "Two beautiful children, boy and a girl… they're teen agers, now."

"They're still in Miami, I gather." I said.

"Yes," she said. "The kids didn't want to change schools…and June had to stay and help the lawyers close out their business…the Auker Improvement Company. Unfortunately it's in bankruptcy."

"If I may…what caused it to fail?" I asked.

"Everything I know comes from June. Irwin will not talk about it. She calls every week, but the moment he hears her voice the poor man chokes up. Can't say a word, and I have to take the phone. Irwin's convinced he's a giant disappointment to June and the kids… and everybody else for that matter," she said, reaching in her handbag for a Kleenex, then wiping away the tears. I placed my hand on her slender forearm.

"June says he was putting up small apartments…when they couldn't build them fast enough in Miami. There was boom down there, you know. He borrowed heavily…got in over his head…the market went sour…couldn't re-pay the banks…worked night and day trying to save the business. When it went under, Irwin went with it."

"That must have been a blow," I said.

She nodded and went on. "June told me it got to the point he couldn't function… couldn't eat or sleep… lost weight…wouldn't leave the house…stayed in bed for days on end. Finally she and the children confronted him. They insisted he see a doctor, and he did."

"Irwin told me a little, but not much," I said.

"Yes. I have plenty of room. I'm his aunt, and he's welcome to stay as long as he wants… or needs to" she said.

"I'm guessing he drove up here by himself."

"He did… thirteen hours… all the way from Miami, Florida. When the poor man pulled into my driveway, he couldn't get out of the station wagon… sat there gripping the steering wheel with both hands. It was all Florence and I could do to get him inside and upstairs to a bedroom.

"It's true," she averred. "He then took to bed for days...wouldn't bathe or dress. Florence and I had to beg him to eat," pausing as if arranging her words. "I tell you, Jason, I've seen a lot in my seventy-three years, but I've never seen a man as utterly defeated as Irwin. I'm speaking in terms of mind, body, and spirit," she said, her bright, empathetic eyes filling with tears.

"It's very sad. He's such a good man... beautiful family... did so well in Miami for so long... went through all that terrible fighting in the war. Now, at times you can push him over with a feather," she said, sadly shaking her head.

"But, Miss Nevaada, from what I've seen, he's feeling better," I said, trying to offer encouragement.

Taking me by the arm, the dear soul agreed. "Thank goodness... he seems to be coming out of it. And thank you for befriending him. Encourage him whenever you can," she said, before turning and walking away, unhurriedly, as if pondering her every step.

Why Auker's cerebral pulse had begun beating again, I did not know. But I paused and pondered the puzzle. Like a fire that can't be put out, my earlier inference continued flaming up from the facts. If we are social creatures—a proposition I had just begun to grasp— then Irwin's meager entry into Hudson's daily life via coffee hour was something of an antidote for his atrocious suffering.

For me that was a good thing. He and I were becoming friends, real friends, "stone buddies" as Dad would say. They're hard to come by you know; at least that's been my experience. No one thing drew me to him. I liked his manliness, precise speech, and innate sincerity, and God knows he was loaded with that. But for whatever reasons, as his mental load began to lift allowing him to reach out to others and others to him, our friendship gelled. We shared an interest in politics and relished assessing candidates, campaigns, and elections. A serious reader, I learned, of books and newspapers, he possessed astute insight and advanced every conversation he entered. One afternoon, unexpectedly, he showed up at the farm and requested "the plantation tour." I was honored. We hopped in a farm truck and spent the better part of the day covering every acre and cross fence on the whole place. It was the first of several such visits, followed by dinner at Dad's place in town, and stimulating talk lasting long into the evening.

Which raises a point. I have my reasons after all these years for telling you about Irwin Auker. I'm hoping the revelations will purge, if not totally then mainly, queries that continue nagging my conscience. Remember, I told you I've tried to forget some of this. Well, here are the questions: In light of our friendship, ephemeral though it was, did I somehow fail the guy? Was there something I could have done? Should have done but did not? For instance, why was it that once he returned to Miami, I kept silent from my end? Would communication, in some form or another, have made any difference whatsoever?

Consider this. It was the attentive Alvin, not me, who suggested we invite Irwin to the one gathering we valued above all others—the monthly meeting of The Clay Cove Supper Club. We were leaving coffee hour one morning when he leaned close and asked, "What about Auker for the Supper Club? We meet next week, you know."

"Absolutely," I replied, annoyed I hadn't thought of it myself.

The Clay Cove Super Club, the only one of its kind in the entire section, was an old-time stag social club. Organized in the 1920s, it existed solely for the pleasures of camp cooking, strong spirits, fellowship, and card games, namely stud poker. The Club met like clockwork on the second Tuesday of each month at one of the most picturesque and my favorite spots in Hurley County—Yancey's Lodge, a splendid cypress-log-pitched-roof structure stationed among aged oak trees on a high bluff above a big bend in the Cypress River. Fifty feet below, the river's coffee-colored waters glided slowly south-southeast toward its terminus with the Atlantic Ocean, thirty-five miles away. Always for guests a few highly valued slots were open.

Neither surprised nor elated, Irwin accepted the invitation. So the following Tuesday night he and I drove down to Yancey's Lodge. When we pulled off the main road and passed through the unlocked iron gate, entered the property, and approached the lighted lodge, we could hear the steady hum of men's voices. Brought together by the vagaries of fate, position, origins, time, and place, members and guests were following the protocols that never varied.

All was in order. The cook committee, clad in white aprons, readied thick t-bones for the grill. Ralph, the black bar tender, attired in his customary white waist coat and black bowtie, was doing a brisk business. Beneath the lodge's high ceilings and hand-hewn rafters, members and guests mixed and mingled, drank and talked and laughed, surrounded by pine-paneled walls the color of fine leather, festooned with largemouth bass, deer heads, wild ducks, and fading framed photographs of hunting parties, marksmen, and smiling fishermen holding long strings of fish. The social hour was at full tilt.

Looking back, I'm convinced that was the night the real Irwin Auker began becoming himself again. He declined a whiskey took a Coke instead and was hesitant, at first. But following Alvin's and my cursory introductions he took hold and waded in, edging deeper and wider, shaking hands right and left, introducing himself, greeting one then another, smiling all the while. Though a stranger to many, he was enjoined, welcomed, and received by a body in which airs and affectations were as foreign as Nikita Khrushchev. At one point he burst out with a full-throated laugh. I heard it myself and marked it a good omen on a memorable evening.

Rung by rung, he continued climbing. Animation replaced the stone-faced stare. Holding the cigarette lighter, his hands no longer trembled. He gained more weight and looked neater and healthier than ever. At coffee hour, communion replaced reticence, as he shifted positions from the outer to the inner circle and became as loquacious as the next. It did not stop there.

Everywhere around Hudson he entered in and pitched in and his station wagon became a common sight. He volunteered at the public library, solicited funds for Community Chest, joined the Lions Club and the Men's Bible Class at First Baptist Church and began attending services. On the opening afternoon of dove season, a near-sacred event for us bird hunters, Irwin showed up wearing Uncle Thornton's Filson game vest and bearing his vintage L. C. Smith double-barrel twelve gauge. He proved a crack shot, taking a limit of sixteen birds, including a number of doubles—a kill with each barrel. It was an admirable feat where I came from. Afterwards, when we gathered for drinks at the tailgate of a pickup, in the stillness and fading light of the winter afternoon, Irwin, gracious and at ease, received compliments all around on his superb shooting. I saw it as further evidence that my new friend—you can't have too many the years have taught me—had overcome the emotional impairments that overwhelmed him somewhere in Miami.

Nothing in his behavior indicated otherwise, as the weeks and months came and went and the seasons changed from fall to winter, to spring, to summer, leading to dog days and the relentless heat of a Georgia August. Then, as I learned is often the case for persons coping with nervous illness, Irwin suffered a bad setback.

It began during Sunday morning services in the sanctuary of First Baptist Church. As had become our custom, he and I were sitting in the same pew next to each other. Reverend Perkins opened with prayer. The congregation sang the first of three hymns. The organist was playing a sedate version of "How Firm a Foundation," and the deacons were passing the oval collection plates. Suddenly I sensed Irwin was unsettled. He was sitting on the edge of the pew, gripping it with both hands, rigid as a light pole. Sweat dripped from his forehead and his body quivered. From his back pocket he grabbed a white handkerchief and wiped his forehead. Abruptly, he rose and stepped to the side aisle and went out the sanctuary. From instinct, I followed.

From the church steps, I spied a man running full-tilt down the tree-lined sidewalk. It was Irwin. He ran like a lion was chasing him; suit coat flapping beneath lunging arms, red tie floating over his shoulder, legs pumping, leaving his station wagon in the parking lot. Without a backward glance he fled, down the sidewalk, across the railroad tracks, and southward toward Third Street, four blocks distant. Dumbfounded, I watched him turn a corner and disappear.

It was panic in its purest state. But what in God's name was I to do? Stalled athwart the granite steps, I stood in a stasis I lack the words to describe, before creeping like a barn rat back into the sanctuary and onto the pew. In harmonious order the service was proceeding.

Auker went unseen for a week or more. Meanwhile I told no one of the incident—not even Alvin and J. R.— nor did I try reaching Irwin or inquiring of Miss Nevaada. That is, sooner than I did. These memories, as I dig them up, are perplexing. You see for me the things I sought most came late—success, wealth, recognition. I find it ironic that they have sharpened and rendered painful these reflections of my putative omissions.

Finally after a week or more, I blurted out at coffee hour, "Anybody seen Irwin lately?" The answer was a collective "no." When I rode by the church parking lot and noted the station wagon missing, I phoned Miss Nevaada.

"Yes," she answered, "Irwin's here… in the bedroom… won't come out… barely lets Florence in with a tray… eats next to nothing. He's living on coffee and cigarettes."

"Does his wife know?" I asked.

`"Lord, no. He forbids me to tell her. He's already burdened down with so much guilt… where she and the kids are concerned."

"Yes, ma'am, I know. What about a doctor?" I asked.

"Won't allow that either. When I suggested it, he became enraged," she said, her voice weakening. "He's in the same shape he was in when he first got here. And, Jason, I'm too old now to deal with this."

"Is there anything I can do?"

"It might help if you came to see him."

"Will he let me see him?"

"I'll ask."

She called back that afternoon. "He wasn't clear either way, but I think he'll see you. Please come... can't possibly hurt... maybe it will help," she said.

Night was falling when I drove into her gravel driveway. She met me at the door, wearing over the long skirt a sweater pulled up around her neck, her thin face drawn with concern. "Thank you, Jason," she uttered, leading me to the foot of the carpeted staircase with polished mahogany banisters. Pointing to the upper floor she said, "Second door on the left."

I knocked on the heavy bedroom door. After a second soft knock, he answered, "Yes?" in a lowered voice.

"It's me, Jason. Can I come in?" I asked.

I heard the lock turn and entered a large room with high ceilings, white walls, and heart-pine plank floors. A massive four-poster bed lay unmade. Maroon drapes were drawn tight over the windows. Irwin sat smoking in a winged chair next to a table and lighted lamp, staring directly at me, expressionless. Wearing a black house coat, slippers, and coffee-stained pajamas, he was unshaven, uncombed, and unkempt.

I thrust out a hand. He took it and said, "So, you've come."

"Why, hell yes," I said. "Nobody's seen you. We got worried about you... missed you at coffee hour."

"I can't imagine why."

"Listen to me, Irwin. You've made a lot of friends here in Hudson. People care about you."

"Maybe, "he said. "But I won't have any after last Sunday," then added, "have a seat."

I reached for a chair, pulled up closer, and asked, "What do you mean 'no friends after last Sunday'?"

"You were there, man. You saw how I peeled out of church, disrupting everything," he said, determined it seemed of convincing him and me.

"You disrupted nothing. Oh a head or two may have turned, but that's all. People leave church all the time… for all kinds of reasons," I said.

"Okay," he said, caustically, obviously unconvinced.

"I did follow you outside though… saw you hauling it down the sidewalk. You're pretty fast for a guy your age," attempting a little levity. Seeing none, I asked, "How old are you, Irwin?"

"I'm 48, this month."

Knowing it was chancy but unable to hold back, I asked, "What happened last Sunday?"

He shifted his weight in the chair, lighted a fresh Pall Mall, and took a long drag. "Aunt Nevaada tells me there's no insanity on either side of the family. If anybody would know she would. But must be going crazy as hell," he said, pointing a straight blunt-tipped finger to his temple.

"I don't believe that for a minute. Why do you say that?" I said, astonished.

"Because. In church last Sunday this outrage took hold of me... blindsided me... that I was about to leap to my feet and start shouting obscenities. I tried to shake it and couldn't. It was like a recorder was turned on in my brain. The thought of such a thing horrified me. My heart began pounding... felt giddy... throat shut tight... started sweating... certain I was losing control. Imagine! Standing up in a church full of people and shouting 'Fuck.' All I could think of was getting the hell out of there. When I reached the sidewalk I ran... and I'm goddamned ashamed of it." Leaning closer he declared, "I tell you it's insanity,"

Was I the audience of a mad man? What in hell was the source of such torment and pain?

"Have you thought about seeing somebody, a professional maybe?" was all I could think of at the time.

Whether he sought or received professional help, I never knew and did not ask. In any event, Irwin again bested his demons and overcame the setback. As the weeks passed he re-appeared with regularity at coffee hour, cleaned up and freshly dressed—to my delight and that of others.

He resumed his duties as a full-fledged civic volunteer, and once more he and the station wagon were visible on the streets of Hudson. Said J. R. Jones at coffee hour, "Boys, Auker's back."

As far as anyone could tell, he was. And then he disappeared, this time for good—free of good-byes, explanations, or notices. Calls, cards, and letters emanated from neither direction, Miss Nevaada excepted. According to her, June sensed her husband was well again and urged him to return to Miami; that she and the children missed and needed him. She said, "Irwin told me, 'I've got my health back and I'm going home' and, of course, he did."

In our final visit a few weeks before her death, weak and failing Miss Nevaada whispered from her bed, I holding her hand, that Irwin and the family were intact. He was back in business erecting and renting convenient stores. As her strength waned she said, "June tells me things are not going well. He's borrowed lots of money... he's worrying again."

From then on, he existed in memory only. Until a cold January morning at coffee hour a year or so later when Hal yelled from his tiny cluttered office at the rear of the station, "Jason, you've got a long- distance phone call."

Hal handed me the receiver, and the caller asked if I was Jason Stoddard.

"I am."

"Mr. Stoddard, I'm Sergeant Jake Walton of the Miami Police Department."

"All right."

"We're investigating what looks like a murder-suicide down here, in a private residence. We found a card lying on the kitchen table. Your name and this number were on it with a note to call you. May I ask you a few questions?"

"Yes...but...first...who are you talking about?"

"A Mr. Irwin Auker and his wife, June."

"What! For God's sake, man, what happened?"

"Mr. Auker sent the kids on an errand to get them out of the house. He then shot his wife and himself with a revolver. They were lying on the floor, clutching each other like lovers in an embrace," he said, in a matter-of-fact yet empathetic voice.

"Officer, you are relaying some very bad news," was all I could utter, darkness I had never known instantly coming over me.

"I know and I'm sorry. This will only take a few minutes," he replied.

His questions were limited and perfunctory. I answered to the extent of my knowledge, handed the receiver back to Hal, and walked away.

The Origins of a Congressman 1982

Preface

This story is based on actual events that occurred in the State of Georgia during the closing weeks of 1981. It expresses the author's conception of the participants and the occasion, parts and pieces of which are true to the occurrence. Other segments are products of the author's imagination. It is for reading as a work of fiction, a short story, not a historic document. To prevent embarrassment for those positively or adversely affected at the time (some of whom are still alive), names of persons and locations are disguised.

Athens, Georgia, April 2012

The unforeseen call came on a busy afternoon in his Baldwin City law office. Sister-in-law, Jan McCurdy, was ringing from his brother's seven-hundred-fifty-acre working farm in Hawkins County ninety miles to the west. Her voice had an anxious edge.

"Did you see the news?" she asked, adding before he could speak. "They've redrawn the congressional districts and moved Hawkins County into the Tenth."

"I saw where the Legislature's reapportioning the districts," he answered. "I didn't see anything about Hawkins County," annoyed he had overlooked it. A member of state and county Democratic committees, he was supposed to stay informed.

She continued, "It's been in all the local papers and on TV. We're going into the Tenth—and that's not all. Bradford Hughes announced he's leaving Congress to run for Governor."

"I know about Hughes. He's always wanted to be governor of Georgia," he said.

"I'm trying to persuade Barry McCurdy to run for Hughes's seat," she stated, lowering her voice.

"Barry? Running for Congress? Jan, are you serious?" he asked, startled, as if someone had fired a pistol in the halls of the law firm.

"I'm dead serious," she replied. "I sat down last week and wrote 'em a letter. I put down every reason I could think of why he can do it—if he will—and why he ought to. He'd never thought of such a thing, but he hasn't dismissed the idea either—so far."

"That's heavy stuff—running for Congress," he said, straining for clarified thoughts. "It's not like a race for probate judge. Congress is big-league politics!" he exclaimed, then blurting, unthinkingly, later regretting it, but forever conscious of the soaring costs of American electioneering. "Where in God's name would we get the money?"

"I don't know, yet," she replied, "but there's got to be a way. Look, John, you and I aren't political imbeciles—we've both worked for congressmen—we know people contribute to candidates they like. And, your brother's one likeable man."

"Correct—on all counts," he admitted.

"Will you think about it?"

"Absolutely."

"Barry needs your encouragement, I need your encouragement, we're up against it.

We've got to try something. I can't tell you how bad things are out here. The farm economy's sinking, and we're sinking with it." With that he heard the receiver click.

He entered the call on his desk book—December 5, 1981.

Jan McCurdy was no old-fashioned isolated farm wife. She was a modern woman, with ingrained interests and a penchant for politics. It stemmed from her background. Before marrying Barry, she worked in the Washington office of Congressman Hamilton Jones, a Republican from Georgia's Third District. Her Grandfather, Sterling Martin, served three terms as Mayor of Columbus. John McCurdy never discounted the opinions of his bright, attractive, upbeat sister-in-law—a Republican among McCurdy Democrats. No happenstance it was she who first saw for her husband a tenable opening.

In brotherhood, John and Barry McCurdy were close; in appearance, temperament, and outlook, they were remarkably dissimilar. John, a conscientious lawyer, was instinctively pessimistic, forever alert—if not expectant—for unwanted results. Jury verdicts in a long string of trials had signified that favorable outcomes in contested matters are rarely guaranteed. A partner in his firm with a heavy workload, he somehow found time for party politics, an interest going back to his time as a Congressional assistant. Aside from work on Democratic committees, he gave occasional speeches at civic clubs, published newspaper essays, and wrote letters to the editor—when issues aroused him.

Barry, easy going and optimistic by nature, had demonstrated an unmistakable flair for farming. Beginning in 1973, he had converted his place from cow pastures to peak production in soybeans, corn, and tobacco. A progressive farmer in a nation of the world's most progressive, he was rising in the leadership of two state-wide farm organizations. That was John's image of his younger brother: American fanner; well-liked upright citizen; good husband and father, one whose political sentiments were non-partisan, in the main subdued.

As for Jan's plea that he 'think about it,' she had no need for worry. The idea bored into McCurdy's brain like an auger. It became a fixation, a chain of non-stop racing contemplations that distracted him at work and awakened him at night. Ill-advised? A bid assured of failure? A farmer with no background in politics? Preposterous?

These were dominant sentiments—at first. But the seed germinated, sprouted, and began lifting the foundations of doubt. "It might be possible after all," he mused, cognizant that the rough-and-tumble world of elective politics contains a bottomless repository of possibilities, realized and abandoned.

His musings were forceful enough and positive enough to support a search for supporting facts. Affirmative evidence lay close by.

Like their father, Barry possessed a god-given capacity for friendship. Wherever time and events carried him, he left a train of devoted friends. A first cousin, with a twinge of envy, once said, "People like the damn guy."

Forever at ease in the presence of strangers, an aptitude for mixing and mingling in groups and crowds are political assets at every level. "A plus for brother," thought John.

Furthermore, as Jan indicated, Barry may have pressing needs for seeking income off the farm. That was understandable. Beginning with the collapse in 1819, American agriculture was plagued with cycles of boom and bust. Each swept off the land vast numbers of broke and bankrupt farmers. The current crash was simply the latest. Jan's phone call, however, was first notice Broad Acres Farm may be in trouble.

People seek elective office for countless reasons. Irrepressible necessities are rarely of interest to the electorate. Absent fraud or scandal, voters gravitate toward the candidate's politics, party, and persona. Barry's strained net worth—if in fact that were the case—amounted to no disqualification, John inferred.

Moreover, on Jan's urgings it may precipitate a final decision, and the sooner the better. The new year was only weeks away. Thereafter, congressional candidates would begin canvassing the district in earnest.

In the interim, at the public library, he inspected the Tenth's demographics, found in the reference work, *A Guide to Georgia Counties*. The district covered a substantial slice of Georgia. It comprised the coastal areas of Sea Islands, where the great rice and cotton plantations disappeared after the Civil War and the abolition of slavery. Its northern tip lay thirty-five miles south of Augusta. From there it stretched south and westward to the Florida line, a distance of 210 miles. Its twenty counties were home to 527,732 citizens, of whom 180,225 or 34.2 percent were African-American. Registered voters numbered 218,839 or 40.5 percent of the population.

The greater numbers lived in small towns and rural areas. Baldwin City, by far, was the largest municipality with 77,000 residents. The citizenry, rural and urban, was overwhelmingly Protestant and of Scotch-Irish descent. Agriculture and forestry were the district's leading industries. If he offers, John surmised, the electorate fits both Barry's farm appeal and his urban, experience. Another favorable factor.

The demographics registered a further truth he was quick to see. The Tenth was big. Those electioneering to represent it faced lots of ground to cover, people to meet, and hands to shake.

Days passed without further word from the farm. The following Saturday, however, McCurdy drove to Satilla County and the Town of Hudson, population 900, for a routine visit with the McCurdy brothers' aging parents. Satilla and Hawkins were adjoining counties, bounded by the slow-flowing, coffee-colored water of the Cypress River. Along for the ride that day, for the conversation and view of the countryside was his good friend, Chris Reading.

Their visits over, preceded by a fine lunch and filled with Martha McCurdy's renowned pound cake, the two were seated in John's station wagon for their return to Baldwin City. Barry suddenly pulled beside them in a heavy, dust coated farm truck. Rolling down the window, he inquired if they could stop by the farm on the way home. When both answered, yes, he said, "I need to talk to both of you," his tanned face pinched and solemn, then driving away. They followed at a distance.

Reading, a corporate lawyer in a Baldwin City firm and a moderate Republican, shared John's interest in politics. A voracious reader and close observer of current events, he was imbued with intense acuity. His antennae constantly scanned the horizon at high frequency, giving him a feel and sense of the times. Every conversation he entered moved a step forward.

Reading and his wife, Mimi, had become acquainted with Barry and Jan on social occasions. When John related

Jan's phone call during the short drive to the farm, certain it was the reason Barry wanted to see them, Reading's, response was instantaneous. "That's exciting. Barry strikes me as a damn good man. He just might make a good candidate." Thinking aloud, he went on. "This is how it always begins. Somebody, somewhere, wants to go public, or continue in office if he has one. When ambition overpowers impediments—and there's always plenty of 'em—he has to talk about it. He can't help it. Politics is no game for the silent."

John concurred. "I expect those who want to run in eighty-two are already talking about it."

"No doubt," said Reading

On the road ahead, the travelers could see the windbreaks, fields, and rust-colored barn on Broad Acres Farm. The sturdy, yellow 1866-style farmstead and surrounding acreage fronted Highway 38 for half a mile. John McCurdy slowed and made a left-hand turn onto the dirt lane leading to the house. Both travelers savored the political meeting they envisioned and welcomed it.

As they predicted, other aspirants in this preliminary period of Tenth District politics would hold their concealed gatherings. None, however, would leave deeper impressions on the participants or prove as fateful as the one about to begin on Broad Acres Farm.

Those wishful of succeeding Bradford Hughes would survey the scene, inventory resources, and gauge their chances. Irrespective of where, when, or how conducted, their probes reflected the reality that elective office in America is open to those who have the will to seek it. Their numbers are few. Contrary to popular belief, citizens capable of casting their bread on the choppy waters of the body politic comprise a miniscule, icy-nerved minority.

Absent an overriding national debate, some agitation of local interest, or factions with an ox to gore, congressional elections are fought out at the grassroots. Their outcomes are heavily influenced by a provincial web of influence, unperceived by the everyday electorate. The web embraces local officials, prominent citizens, family ties, blood relations, business contacts and connections. Its influence drips into the race like a chef dropping ingredients in a simmering stew. Low in the early going, then rising and gathering force, the web's influence becomes known as Election Day nears and voters respond to its candidate of choice—the one who knew, or learned how, to reach it in the right way.

Theodore White wrote in his narratives of American politics, "In no other country can so few galvanize so many. In no other country can the rank amateur—on his own initiative, self-appointed and self-proclaimed—assemble whatever resources he can and launch a drive for elective office with greater chance of success."

McCurdy and Reading were aware of these truths. Experienced lawyers, they knew, too, that as there is no one way for an advocate to put his case to a jury no two congressional elections are identical. Candidates must accommodate and adjust to the continuing factors of personality, social, economic, and technological change.

Singly, and in combination, the foregoing verities would influence the discussions about to commence at the McCurdy farmstead.

The visitors parked in rear of the house, amid pickup trucks, a rubber-tired grain combine, and tractors the size of army tanks. As they walked toward the back door, John looked at his watch; it was two o'clock. A shroud of grayness covered the early-winter sky, a light mist was falling, and it was turning colder. Smoke rose from the massive brick chimney that anchored the rear of the house, before floating downward and drifting close across the earth. Save calls of a far-off crow, at Broad Acres Farm quietness and an unfettered stillness prevailed.

When his visitors entered, Barry greeted them sideways, bent before the huge fireplace laying on the flames a fresh piece of oak.

From the open kitchen at the opposite end of the long room, Jan called out, "Welcome, John and Chris. I'll have coffee in a minute." In a matter of moments, she stepped out wearing loafers, a denim skirt, and crisp white shirt, carrying a tray with cups, saucers, and a pot of black coffee spiked with chicory. Pouring a first round of the elixir that stimulates thought and sharpens wits, she reported their sons, Barry, Jr., 12, and Bill, 10, were away with friends.

The four assembled in a room furnished for informal living, one that served as dining room and den. The fireplace, wide hearth, and heart-pine mantle abutted the north wall. Arrayed in front were a sofa and comfortable arm chairs. Here and there lay the paraphernalia of small boys: a football, a bag of rocks, a turtle's shell, a Red Ryder BB gun leaning against the wall.

Hosts and guests, instinctively at ease one with another, ceased polite talk to enjoy the coffee, the presence of each other, the moment. Flames crackled in the fireplace and barely audible was the hum of traffic on Highway 38. From the room's windows, the scene was of open fields bordered by pine and hardwood forests. In former times, thought John, as he sipped Jan's strong brew and gazed across the property, men and mules tilled those fields. That was long before a mechanical, electrical, and scientific revolution enveloped the American farm. He once read in a statistical abstract that in 1940, 5,400 gas-powered tractors were at work on Georgia farms. By 1950 there were 85,000.

The interlude was transitory. Barry led them toward the fireplace, and their parley began.

Jan, John, and Reading settled into the easy chairs and sofa. Barry remained standing, his back to the flames. Dressed in worn jeans, work boots, and a starched chambray shirt, clean shaven, thick hair freshly brushed, he looked younger than his thirty-nine years. To John, he appeared much too thin and exuded an uncharacteristic somber air.

"I suspect you know that Jan thinks I ought to run for Congress," said Barry, opening the dialogue. "The woman wrote me a two-page letter to that effect—*hand delivered it, mind you.* I've stopped counting the times I've read it. Frankly, I've never considered running for office—until now. But the truth of the matter is I am considering it. Both of you know politics. All due respect to Jan, but is the idea feasible?

"You haven't heard all I've got to say on this subject, either," Jan declared firmly.

"Now's the time, dear. You're not excluded," Barry replied.

"Chris and I want to hear from you, Jan. You're the reason we're all here,," said John.

"Well this I can tell you," asserted Jan, emphatically. "I've seen a lot of politics—been around politics and plenty of Congressmen. I know my husband. I know how he relates to people—all kinds of people. Barry can do it. I'm certain of it."

"I respect your opinions, Jan—always, and I'm inclined to agree with you on this one," said John. "But you and I are biased witnesses. Shouldn't we try looking at this thing as disinterestedly as we can? There's some big implications here," said John.

"Yes we should," agreed Barry. "I want everything laid on the table, being that I may become the sacrificial lamb."

Jan nodded concurrence.

"As I see it, people," John continued, looking around, "the question is not how Barry ought to run a campaign, or ought to run his office—if elected. Since he's made no decision yet, I say we address the feasibility of his making a bid in the first place?"

"Exactly," said Barry.

"If I may," said Reading. "Anybody thinking about running for public office can always find a dozen reasons *not to run*. The trick is to find one good reason *to run*."

"We've got a damn good one—low farm prices," exclaimed Jan.

With that, there was laughter all around.

"It will help us, I think, to know how you feel about it, Barry," suggested John. "From the top down, so to speak. Tell us, if you will, and include some background—for Chris's benefit," choosing his words carefully, wanting no resentment from a younger brother, who then and always was his own person.

"Gladly," Barry responded, grateful for the opportunity. "Frankly, I haven't thought of much else these past few days."

For the three who heard it, the statement that followed was deeply influential. He opened standing in place and continued, the commentary broken by a remark or a question, pausing from time to time to sip from the cup Jan unobtrusively refilled. Throughout he spoke in a conversational tone, sometimes sitting briefly on the hearth.

He began by asserting belief in the country's institutions and his own respect for the Office of U.S. Representative. There was much to learn, but he held no doubt of its power and influence, its ways and means of serving both the Tenth District and the nation. The more he dwelled on the position, the greater its appeal. A seat in congress was worth the striving.

He spoke of his family background, of its deep roots in the section, of his upbringing in the small farm town of Hudson. He described his education there, beginning in the public schools and later at the University of Georgia, where he was elected Commander of the Sigma Nu social fraternity.

In an aside, he conjectured he was the only full-time farmer in Georgia with a degree in English literature.

Again, there was more laughter.

His forbearers were among the early settlers of Satilla and Hawkins counties, beginning in the first decades of the nineteenth century. Mostly, they were farmers, tradesmen, mechanics, and small land owners—decent, law-abiding citizens. A number of their direct descendents still lived in the area.

A few had distinguished themselves. Grandfather Henry McCurdy, was a large land owner, cotton ginner, and banker. Great Uncle Willard Murphy, the son of original Irish immigrants, grew up in Hawkins County, found a job in Baldwin City, and later became president of its principal bank. Great Uncle Ira McCurdy moved to Sarasota in the 1920s, grabbed hold of the Florida land boom and made a fortune in the lumber business.

With feeling and affection, he described his and Jan's marriage, their two small sons, and their early married years in Baldwin City, where he worked in Uncle Willard's bank and later as a retail stock broker. When the market went sour and he inherited the farm, he moved the family to Hawkins County and began farming the place. That was in 1973.

Their years in Baldwin City were good ones. He and Jan enjoyed the active, vibrant, social world of young people, many of whom were sons and daughters of prominent families. They made many friends, some of whom he called by name. Like their parents, they were very conservative and Republican. Historically, the city claimed a substantial Republican contingent.

Jan broke in politely adding, "Besides our social friends, we know a lot of other people. We've got lots of contacts down there."

Unomitted was his relationship with the African-American citizenry. Since earliest memory, he had lived and worked among them. He held no prejudice whatsoever and claimed numerous blacks as friends and acquaintances. On his father's farm, he once dove into a pit well and rescued a black youth who had fallen in, unable to swim. No barriers would prevent his mixing with black voters, in all settings.

He paused and asked of their numbers in the Tenth. "According to the *Guide to Georgia Counties*, that number is 218,000 plus," answered John.

As for politics, he espoused no radical views and was not one for extreme statements. On national issues, he claimed neither knowledge nor expertise beyond those of the average citizen save one: American agriculture—an industry basic to the economy and heavily influenced by government policy. Here, he expounded more specifically.

When he began farming, it was a recorded fact; America was the greatest exporter of farm commodities in world history. Sales of wheat to Russia expanded foreign markets still further. Across the '70s farm prices and farm income rose steadily. Land prices escalated to unheard of levels. He, and farmers throughout the country, with easy credit from The Federal Land Bank, leveraged their assets. They bought more land, machinery, and equipment and went heavily into debt, exhorted all the while by Secretary of Agriculture, Earl Butz, to "plant fence row to fence row." The decade saw a massive modernizing, upgrading, and expansion of U.S farm capacity. Governor Nelson Rockefeller of New York, then a candidate for President, said, "Agriculture is America's growth industry." And it was.

Farmers' spirits were high. Farm organizations were active, and he and Jan joined in. As a result, he was acquainted with individual farmers in many of the Tenth's rural counties. He had visited their farms, attended their parties, joined in their hunts. Some he identified by name and county of residence.

As the decade neared its turn, however, the farm prosperity wave broke and fell back. The first salvo was fired on the Texas gulf coast when union labor raised a furor over non-union longshoremen loading wheat aboard cargo

ships bound for Russia. Then along came President Jimmy
Carter, a peanut farmer from Plains, Georgia. On January
4, 1980, he embargoed sales of grains to the Soviet Union,
letting loose once more the cycle of boom and bust.

As he described the collapse that followed, Barry's
voice emitted bitterness. Farm exports plummeted. Massive surpluses of soybeans, corn, cotton, and rice began
accumulating. The USDA was predicting that by November of the coming year it would store 3.4 billion bushels
of surplus corn, half the year's crop. On the heels of the
embargo, farm prices fell, and farm income dropped precipitously. For the first time since 1946, the price for an
acre of Georgia farm land had fallen. Having floated up
on the flood of good times, the farm economy was coming
down hard, unseen for half a century. The bust had imperiled and outraged heavily leveraged producers at every
country crossroads in America. On the issues affecting
agriculture, he welcomed a chance to be heard.

On that point, he rested. He asked Jan for a fresh cup
and said, "There you have it. Tell me what you think, and
don't hold back."

John McCurdy recognized in his brother's statement
an admirable depth of thought and expression. Still further it deepened his belief in Barry's political potential. "I
liked what I heard," he said, nodding toward Barry, who
smiled in return.

Taken in by McCurdy's presentation, Reading had put
aside his coffee and kept notes throughout (hurriedly jotted

and retained for years). Scanning them now, he volunteered approval. "Well done, Barry," he said. "And, I'm in total agreement about Carter's embargo. Even the untutored could see it was an economic and diplomatic disaster."

"Farmers are disgusted about it. It took years to open those foreign markets." Barry responded still bitter. "The only thing we got out of Jimmy Carter was a silly grin."

Everyone laughed.

Thus ended the afternoon's only colloquy touching on government policy. Thereafter, they aimed thoughts and comments at the core question.

"First things first, y'all," said Jan. "Now that you've heard Barry, don't you agree he's got something to offer?"

"Unquestionably," answered Reading. "A candidate needs to be presentable, and articulate, to some extent anyway. Barry's solid on both points," pausing before enumerating jokingly. " You may not be Rock Hudson, Barry, but you pass the public appearance test with flying colors."

"Thank you," retorted Barry.

"And, here's something else to consider," said Reading. "A run for any public office is hazardous in and of itself. In that regard it's like waging war. The unforeseeable is always out there. But the fact Barry hasn't held office isn't a hazard. Any number of Congressmen won their seats on the first try."

"I agree with both of you," said John. "Barry has the makings of a good candidate. On the stump, appearances do matter. And, Jan, you and Barry and the boys are a beautiful family. You all have public appeal. Undoubtedly that bolsters Barry's viability."

"Very true," added Reading.

"And you're articulate enough. That is if you'll just give the speeches I write for you," said John in false modesty.

"If I throw my hat in the ring, Lawyer McCurdy, I predict you'll come down here and try taking over the campaign," avowed Barry, cracking a slight smile.

"I resent that," John shot back.

"Seriously," said John, "you've never lacked for vigor and you're not afraid of hard work. Believe me, those are critical considerations. Electioneering for Congress is a dawn to exhaustion job. It's taxing in the extreme on mind and body, especially in a district as big as the Tenth. People can't imagine all that's involved in a campaign for high office."

"Just how big is the district?" asked Barry.

"It's huge," John replied, "210 miles from pole to pole, 20 counties, 527,000 souls."

As Barry pondered John's data, Jan sat upright on the sofa, stiff and erect. As she spoke, her jaw quivered. "Yes, it's a big district. And, yes, it would be an immense undertaking. And, yes, we can't sit here this afternoon and predict the outcome. But, dammit, y'all, we're political creatures. Don't overlook that. A McCurdy for Congress campaign sounds exciting to me. Congressional politics can be a lot of fun. I know. I've worked in campaigns.

Think of the interesting people, the towns, counties, and neighborhoods to see and visit, the rallies and the barbecues. Barry can speak out on problems distressing him and hear about the concerns of others. We're talking about the politics that matter. And they're removed from this piece of dirt we live on, where we'll soon be broke, which is where we're going." Her shoulders slumped, her eyes watered, as she reached for a Kleenex in her handbag.

His wife's words resonated. Barry turned and reached for a long iron poker and began stirring up the fire logs. Reading, silent, looked over his notes.

John stared at his sister-in-law with enhanced respect before breaking silence. "Not for a minute do I dispute one word you say, Jan," he said empathetically.

Reading renewed the parlance with interrogatories to Barry. "Let's move to the next point. Mind taking a personal question or two?" he asked.

"I do not," answered Barry shaking his head, "ask me everything you can think of."

"How old are you?"

"I'm thirty-nine."

"The ideal age. You're old enough to have plenty of experience and young enough to have years of life expectancy," declared Reading moving to the next one. "Don't take offense, but are there any hidden liabilities, skeletons, something, or somebody that could come out of the closet and cause embarrassment? Claims of any kind or tax liens for example?"

"No," Barry answered rigidly. "Jan and I have talked about that one. I've paid my taxes. I've obeyed the law, and I haven't tried to screw anybody out of anything in my life. Nothing's lurking in the closet," tacking on meekly, "I may have left behind one or two broken hearts."

"Lots of 'em," shouted Jan.

"Enough said. You're qualified!" pronounced Reading visibly pleased. "Actually you're more than qualified, and I should have brought this out sooner. The only requirements for membership in the House are that one is twenty-five, a citizen for seven years, and an inhabitant of the state where elected. So says the U.S. Constitution."

Their discourse went from there, John speaking next. "I see something here that should prove beneficial," he averred. "You've got a dual connection. Barry's profile fits the Tenth's electorate to a T. He's Protestant, a famer, and a native with deep roots. Yet, he has also lived and worked in the district's big city. Complimentary factors only—I admit. But trust me; they can set him apart from the opposition that's forming up. The duality may not win a lot of votes, but it won't lose him any either. They're like the courtroom lawyer's grooming and dress. They won't win the case for him, but they sure as hell can lose it."

"As for Baldwin City," said Barry, "I want to think our friends down there will support me. That's despite the fact most of 'em, and their families, are staunch Republicans. There's no question they're very conservative."

"In a grassroots election, friendship often times trumps a voter's politics. Provided the candidate makes the right pitch," responded John confidently.

Her composure regained, Jan chimed in. "Barry Mc-Curdy knows how to make that right pitch. Gets along great with people—makes friends like nobody I've ever seen," smiling and winking at her husband, who sat on the red brick hearth taking in the colloquy as efficiently as his John Deere combine harvested a field of standing corn.

"That's more bonus points for you Barry," said Reading. "That's what Tip O'Neal meant when he said, 'All politics is local.'"

"Bear with me, everybody. It's the lawyer in me coming out," said John, scanning hastily scratched notes. "We've been at it for some time. Let's give our inquiry a little structure. It seems to me we've developed certain postulates." He gave them out in sequence.

First, by reason of age, family appeal, deep roots hereabout, clean record, people skills—and his speaking skills—our man, Barry, has the essential tools for a viable candidacy. The response was an obvious, "yes."

Second, his dual connections with the city and the rural counties are advantageous. Again, agreement.

Third, Barry's profile and occupation are a good fit among Tenth District voters. Another, "yes."

Barry raised his hand with a comment. "While you're at it," he said, "you might as well throw this one on the pile with the rest of 'em—I am *not* a lawyer."

"Received and accepted," declared John, laughing heartily, then inquiring, "I'm assuming if you run you'll do so as a Democrat."

"Right," replied Barry. "Momma and Daddy are Democrats. Always have been. You are, too. I can't see myself as a Republican, although I've voted for some of 'em."

"As of this very hour, I'm no longer a Republican either," declared Jan.

"Then we have Postulate Four," concluded John. "The first hurdle on the road to Washington is the trial by fire in the July Democratic Primary."

Reading alluded to Hubert Humphrey on primaries, who reportedly said, "Primaries are a bitch. I'd rather be put on the rack than run in a primary election." Thus, the primary became the topic of discussion.

The primary election is unique to American democracy, where power of the federal government is divided three ways. Hubert Humphrey was not alone in his dread of them. Politicians of every stripe share his sentiment and for good reason. Primary contests suck up money from contributors who are best tapped in the general election. They often furnish the opposition ammunition to use against the winner in the general election. Worst of all, they can exhaust the candidate, mentally and physically, while draining his finances.

Others with a dislike for party primaries, whose support the office-seeker is compelled to solicit, include local officials, party activists, and politicos with political friends.

They detest having to declare preferences or loyalties before facing the real enemy in the general election. Candidates can expect to hear repeatedly the old saw, "I can't commit to you, but I won't work against you."

It rarely calls for elaborate oratory. Short set speeches and pithy phrases are all that's necessary in Congressional primaries in 1982 and were bound to be waged among ordinary people. Television was yet to become today's juggernaut. For most candidates, it would be first contact, the first direct appeal. He is well advised to make his approach close to the grassroots, but at a distance that portrays him as a dignified law maker. The better strategy is to refrain from beheading primary opponents. The defeated may agree to help the winner in the general election.

"We get the message," said Barry. "I have no misgivings about what's in store, that is if I'm in it."

"Okay," said John, looking up from his notes, "if Barry enters, he's got to win by the primary route and that means showing strength early, including the ability to raise money."

Said Reading, "The reality is you can't wage a campaign without money, and they're growing more expensive in every cycle. The sooner you can raise funds, the better. There's the saying in politics, 'Early money is the sweetest.' The media's quick to characterize a candidate's fundraising as a measure of strength, or weakness."

"I don't question that, Chris, but I'd like to hear about the opposition. Who will I have to run against?" inquired Barry with renewed firmness.

Jan joined in, "If there's somebody out there you see as unbeatable, we need to know about it."

"Right. The last thing this family needs is a lost cause," emphasized Barry.

"I understand," John interposed. "It's true. Some people *are* unbeatable. Some races are unwinnable, but the eighty-two race in the Tenth ain't gonna be one of 'em. There'll be no incumbent in this one, and incumbents start out with a distinct advantage. Furthermore, no steamroller prospect's out there mulling an entry. If there were, I would have heard."

"I agree," said Chris. "But Barry's right, too. It's time we look at the lineup. John, you take the Dems. I'll throw out a line on the Republicans."

Admitting the party grapevine and his law firm's contacts were sources of intelligence, John complied. Among Democrats there was one confirmed candidate, and he looked upon the Hughes seat in Congress as his rightful estate. He was Aaron Chandler, State Senator, lawyer, born and reared in Baldwin City. John knew him personally and professionally. They had practiced together for two years as associates at John's firm, before Chandler and another associate withdrew to open their own office. Chandler made no secret of his plans to succeed Hughes. "Bert and I have it all worked out," he would say, a statement McCurdy classified as manifest illusion.

Chandler's election to the Georgia Senate was something of a fluke. He defeated a weak, discredited, clownish incumbent. Still in his first term, his record to date was inconsequential. He came from an old, distinguished, and once-wealthy family that from all accounts had known better times. He was bright, highly educated, honorable, likeable, and fantastically unrealistic. Lethargic and urban to the core, his politics were restricted to the wants and needs of the city and its inhabitants. For Chandler, politics was a process of arrangement among the privileged and well positioned, a process without variation, reservation, contest, or effort. In neither his politics nor persona was the man suited for connecting with rural and small-town voters—or they with him. Shortcoming number one.

His second deficiency was a pronounced obliviousness of the stress and strain, the sheer energy requisites, of a congressional race. If so, the man had insufficient strength and stamina to meet them. Local recognition and home-town support would put Chandler out front in the early going. By no standards, however, was he unbeatable. On the contrary, his inherent weaknesses translated into a flawed contestant, one decidedly vulnerable.

In second place, in terms of punch and potential, and certain to qualify, was State Representative Rufus Ward, a solo lawyer from nearby Marlowe County. Ward was a stock character from an array of American types. Big in girth and manner, rumpled, intensely gregarious, a habitué at local bars and taverns, Ward's everlasting wish was to be liked. Now forty-five, with two failed marriages behind him and children to educate, his small-time law practice barely met his needs. Some months it did not. Similarly, his record in the Georgia House was undistinguished. From having handled legal matters with Ward, John considered his work of average quality. His disjointed public speech reflected either a consistent failure of preparation or the inability to measure up to standards expected from a member of the Bar. A state court judge, long acquainted with Ward, upon learning he was offering for Congress, reacted by saying, "Rufus is so inadequate for that office." Reliable rumor indicated Ward was without financial reserves. All things considered, he would prove weaker than Chandler.

On the fringe, lesser lights were circling. Among them, Randolph Turner, a little-known Juniper County cattle breeder and World War II fighter pilot in the Pacific. He had no political record, but had established an exquisite reputation for eccentricity. Some considered him a crackpot.

Clarence Washington, a black attorney, was once a comer among Baldwin City trial lawyers. He dropped from sight years ago, allegedly due to a rare form of mental illness. No one knew for sure. Those in the know reported he is a shell of his former self. They are astonished he would consider seeking elective office.

Last in the Democratic array was Byron Bartlett, a thirty-year-old businessman from the coastal counties. He, too, had no elective record but had dabbled in party affairs at the local level. Party insiders believe he has promise and have encouraged him to wait for other opportunities. They classify him "unconditioned for a congressional race."

In sum, John saw the Democratic field as wide open and weak. With work and effort Barry was the equal of any, his chances just as good. Timing, therefore, always a factor, leaned in his direction.

Barry reminded his brother he had neglected Herbert Perkins, a district staff man for Hughes. In a local restaurant that very morning, he overheard Perkins was in the contest. One patron swore he had seen a Perkins bumper sticker. Though John had heard nothing of Perkins's plans, he knew the man well and proceeded with an evaluation. At his best, Perkins was as impressive as a grocery sacker. The man was heavy, swarthy, coarse, and ungracious. His manner of representing the Congressman told the tale. He would position himself at the rear of the hall bearing a menacing countenance, drinking, silent, doing nothing, greeting few, and leaving before the program ended. No one understood why Hughes hired the man.

"That's Herbert Perkins for you," declared John emphatically, crashing his fist on the arm of his chair. "If he's a respectable candidate, forget viable, I am King Farouk."

"Well, McCurdy," said Barry with no trace of amusement, "there's another of your 'postulates' we can all agree on. You are not King Farouk."

Reading assumed the floor and reviewed Republican prospects.

Outlook for the GOP was narrow. In Baldwin City, in the Tenth, and across the State, party membership and influence were building. It was expected to offer a candidate in the upcoming race. Ralph Adams, a well-liked, low-key, small-town banker with bona fide Republican credentials was the likely man. Nevertheless, even with Ronald Reagan in the White House, in the Tenth, 1982 was not destined to become a Republican year. The district remained firmly Democratic. Congressman Hughes and his predecessors were Democrats to a man. Moreover, no Republican prospect capable of altering the status quo was anywhere in sight. On that key, Reading rested and sat back in his chair.

John ratified Reading's conclusions. Pointing to Barry and Jan he said, "I trust you two get the drift."

"We do," said Barry, Jan nodding concurrently. "Should we win the primary, our chances look brighter in November,"

"Precisely. Win in July and you'll have the wind at your back," Reading predicted confidently.

"So," said John, "We've got postulate five. The Democrat will go to Congress."

At this point, you could sense it. After a long afternoon of politics, the four were growing weary. Night was falling at the farm, and Barry made no effort to refuel flames in the big fireplace, now burning low. John, seeing mental resources were nearing exhaustion, elected to try for one last point. "It's getting late," he said, "and Chris and I need to be going. Shall we take a quick look at money?"

"Please," answered Jan.

And they tried. What would it take for cards, yard signs, brochures, newspaper and television ads, a campaign staff, gasoline, motel bills, hamburgers, and fresh underwear? No one knew. It was a matter of speculation. They could foresee his facing the electorate three times—in the primary, the primary run-off, and the general election. In the sprawling Tenth, that guaranteed a long campaign that would swallow funds in huge gulps. And that was how they left it.

The young farmer and his supportive wife followed their visitors out into the cold, fresh air and bade them farewell. Facing a decision of profound consequence, they stood side by side, still as statues, faces expressionless, watching the station wagon, its lights on high beam, enter the darkened lane and disappear into the Georgia night.

Epilogue

Three weeks later, in the same setting, on a bright Sunday afternoon, surrounded by his entire family, a collection of close friends, and a smattering of local officials, Barry McCurdy announced he would be a candidate for U.S. Representative. There was a burst of applause.

In early February, Cypress River Technical College sponsored the first public forum for congressional candidates. Martha McCurdy attended and reported to John, "I know it's still early, but I wanted to size up the competition. And I've got news for you; your brother's going to Congress. He's the sharpest man in the race."

Her son did 'go to Congress.' After winning the Democratic primary, he defeated his Republican opponent by a margin of 67,015 to 36,315 votes, carrying every county in the district. He went on to represent the Tenth for five successive terms, declining to seek a sixth.

Caterpillars and Cold Weather

Shadows were growing long on a cold winter Saturday in segregated Hawkins County, and Levi Booth — faithful, unerring employee of the Howe Improvement Company — sat brooding in his modest cottage in the Quarters before a pine-log fire. Sick and out of work the week just ending, he foresaw in the uncommon cold a formidable threat, and it preyed upon his psyche.

Mild winters are the mean in Hawkins County. January temperatures average 51 degrees. Few were aware of the winter of 1917-18 when temperatures plunged to 9 degrees and cypress ponds and drains froze over. Booth, however, knew about it. Once, on an errand to the Courthouse, he overheard old men sitting in cane-bottom chairs describing the Freeze of '18. A weather watcher by nature and necessity, he stood close, listened in, and remembered what he had heard.

Now, in Booth's subtropical section of South Georgia another unwanted hard freeze was on the way. As he stirred the fire logs with an iron poker, black as the color of his skin, he sensed the change. The house was becoming chilled. A frigid wind had begun whistling through window screens and moaning in the pine trees that rose like light poles in the back yard. From the radio in the kitchen, he heard the afternoon forecast: "Cold front moving in. High today thirty. Low tonight fifteen. High tomorrow forty. Check all vehicles for freeze protection."

"Fifteen degrees," thought Booth, "about as bad as that freeze in '18." A big peril for owners of vehicles, trucks, and tractors, unless winterized with anti-freeze. Without it, frozen water would burst blocks and radiators. The question tormenting the conscientious Booth was whether the Improvement Company's four massive Caterpillar tractors had received a dose of anti-freeze. He couldn't be sure either way. "If they didn't, we've got a big problem," concluded Booth.

Though seated as close to the fireplace as he dared, he could not seem to get warm, even when pulling over his narrow shoulders Cora's red and blue handmade quilt. His thighs ached. His back throbbed. Weakness was disabling and deep breaths exuded wheezes and rattles. Since leaving Dr. James's office on Tuesday, he had lain about the house, mainly in bed, arising only to sip rice soup and nibble saltines. He felt inordinately unwell.

A man of spare but lean and sinewy frame, Booth's person bore no distinctive feature, save his large, ambidextrous hands, the palms of which were the color of ivory.

Turned over, they were the color of coal. For two decades of employment in Horace Howe's rise and fall enterprises, Booth's quick mind and nimble hands responded to his superior's every want and need: overhauling combustion engines, driving heavy trucks and trailers, burning and welding, maneuvering skidders, steering band saws, operating draglines, and now bulldozers. The Improvement Company owned four of them — mammoth, mustard-colored diesel-powered Caterpillars, Models D-6. A single machine could do the work of 400 draft horses. They had rolled off the assembly line in Peoria Illinois, then shipped by flatbed trailer to the dealer in Savannah, where Howe acquired them, pledging every asset he owned to finance them. "I work for the Caterpillar Tractor Company," he would say.

Workers at the Improvement Company, of greater or lesser skill and ability, frequently came and went. Not so Booth. He remained steadfastly in place, his services growing ever more valuable. Their's was a two-man fraternity — of labor and loyalty, of duty and sacrifice, of unfailing reciprocal respect. Irrespective of the job, the location, the problems, the hazards, or the weather, their fraternal bonds held firm. And Howe had long since recognized Levi's inherent worth. "The best operator with the best hands in Georgia, black or white," the balding, lanky, restless, entrepreneurial Howe pronounced, repeatedly. His words never reached Booth's ears.

Manifestations of fondness, of regard and appreciation, undoubtedly present and deeply felt, went undeclared. Compliments, handshakes, pats on the back were non-existent. Said Nancy, Howe's observant married daughter, "My father has a great need for affection. He is incapable of expressing it, even to his family, even to the essential Levi Booth. That holds for the entire Howe family. There's something in the genes." Further, the Howe-Booth bonds bridged the segregated social order. Neither questioned it nor sought to circumvent it; they lived it. They shared no meals nor lodging. On overnight road trips Booth found a room in the Quarters. Howe went to the motel. On regular visits to meet with Howe in his big house, Booth entered through the back door, always.

Still bent before the fire, Booth stirred the flames and pondered the night that had fallen filled with risk. He heard the kitchen door open and close and paper sacks with groceries settle on the table. Cora was coming home from work at Howe's residence on 12th Street, where she cooked and cleaned six days a week. She was as plump as he was spare, as light skinned as he was dark, as opinionated and outspoken as he was solemn and dutiful. Contrary to segregation's edict, she insisted on making her way to work through the ponderous front door. No one made an issue of it.

As she entered the room, while removing a grey, waist-length coat, he neither looked up nor spoke. She paused near the fireplace. "Doctor James tole you to stay in the bed," she said.

"I know what he tole me," he replied. "How cold is it outside?"

"It's freezin' and gettin' colder by the minute."

She returned to the kitchen. A large thermometer hung from a rack outside the window, in easy view from the sink. "It's down to twenty-five and fallin'. Weather man said it'll get down to twelve by mornin'," she said, stepping back into Booth's presence.

"Just what I thought," he muttered.

"Tell me what you're thinkin', Levi."

"It ain't what I'm thinkin'; it's what I know. This damn freeze that's comin' will bust every truck and tractor block in Hawkins County, lessen they've got anti-freeze in 'em."

"Don't worry. You put anti-freeze in the pickup outside," said Cora.

"It ain't the pickup I'm worried about, woman. It's those four Caterpillars sittin' down yonder on the Bedford Tract. Without anti-freeze the water in 'em will freeze and expand and split 'em wide open. A disaster for Mistah Howe."

"But don't they have anti-freeze?"

"I cain't be sure. I didn't put it in 'em. One of the other hands may have, but I doubt it. I've heard him say, 'It ain't likely to freeze in Hawkins County and I'm not wasting money on anti-freeze.' You know how close he operates, how he takes chances. Ain't afraid of Black Lucifer hisself."

"That's his problem," said Cora.

"No. It's our problem, too. Let them Caterpillars bust and he'll be ruined. It'll cost a fortune to repair 'em. It'll put him out of business, an' we'll go out with it." After a pause, "An' another thing. Don't forget all he's done for us."

"Yes. An' look at all we've done for him for twenty years or more," said Cora. "So stop worryin', Levi. There's nothin' you can do about those big tractors."

"Oh, yes there is. I can go down yonder an' see if they've got anti-freeze in 'em, an' if they don't, drain the water out, eight gallons a piece."

"You're not goin' out in this freezin' night, Levi," said Cora, becoming adamant and tearful. "You're a sick man already. You'll get pneumonia for certain. An' your natural life is worth more than those tractors."

"I didn't say I was goin' anywhere. I said I could."

"No, but that's what you're thinkin'. I haven't been your wife all these years for nothin'."

"Anybody at the big house?" he asked.

"No. The whole Howe family left for Jacksonville this afternoon. Won't be back 'til late tomorrow. Why cain't you send one of the hands down yonder?"

"'Cause it's Saturday night, now, an' they're all scattered out. You couldn't raise a hand with a search warrant," said Levi.

"I'll find out," declared Cora, grabbing her coat and walking out. Booth heard the kitchen door slam behind her.

As he predicted, her diligent search would uncover no hand willing to bundle up and go down to the job site and the Caterpillars, sixteen miles distant over bad roads. Back home again, she would find the pickup missing and the cottage empty. While she was out, he was left with thoughts of her warnings and oppositions, of his misery and discomfort. She was right, of course. For him to be off in the chilled night air was risky. He feared the consequences and his fears penetrated. They were not deep enough, however, to overcome his devotion to Horace Howe. He thought of all they had been through together: of the men and machines; of long days of action and effort, often under a brutal Georgia sun; of Howe's highs and lows according to the money supply; of his unfailing fairness and impartiality to Booth's blackness. How could he not ward off the man's prospective calamity?

He was confident Cora would find no help. And, he was all but certain no Improvement Company employee had winterized the bulldozers. If they were to be drained, and irrespective of how enfeebled he felt, he knew the troublesome task fell on him. He had never let Horace Howe down. Nor would he this time. He possessed a proven will to bear discomfort. Now he must lean upon it.

If, as somebody said, life comes down to a few moments, this was Booth's moment. He rose from the fireplace, pulled on his only heavy coat, work gloves, a wool hat and crept outside to the mud-stained pickup with no heater, his breath exhaling white vapors. He labored himself into the driver's seat and drove out of town, slowly and cautiously, as if the vehicle were a ship navigating in a narrow harbor.

The bulldozers were parked where the men left them at knocking-off time late Friday afternoon. To reach them Booth must traverse primitive dirt roads with water-filled depressions, deep sandy ruts, and narrow one-lane wooden bridges, always in need of repair. For, you see, the Bedford Tract, all five-thousand acres of it, was situated in the southernmost edge of rural Hawkins County. Maintenance of roads leading to and from was of low priority.

In the ink-black freezing night, Levi's tedious trip exacted almost an hour. But, he made it and found the Caterpillars where he expected. Illuminated in the truck's headlights, strewn with mud and dirt, the huge yellow machines sat side by side, like metal sphinxes. A manifestation of man's highest tool-making capacity, they had become money-makers for Horace Howe. They were the livelihood and the charge of Levi Booth. A man of common sense and a realist to the core, he was aware his condition had worsened. The chest rales were more pronounced, as were the pain and weakness. In addition, he had developed a sharp cough, and in his mouth a bitter taste. Staring still at the ponderous tractors in his headlight beams, he was gripped — for the first time — with the realization that he may cease to exist.

"That fate I might not avoid," he thought, "but I can try and save these machines." Welding his remaining strength to rigid resolution and a ruthless determination, he emerged from the chilled truck, leaving the headlights on, and into the outrageous freezing night. Slowly he made his way to the mute machines, intent on draining the liquid — if only water — from their engine parts and steel veins. (If the affluent was the color of green tea, anti-freeze was present.)

He needed no special tools. Drainage occurred from two discharge valves: one at the radiator, the other on the lower side of the engine block. Small petcocks, rotated by hand, activated the valves. The trick lay in getting to them. Some he could reach standing on the ground. The others forced him to climb up over and around bush arms, crawler tracks and engine cowlings.

"Hope I'm wrong," thought Booth, as he grasped the first petcock. "Maybe somebody put anti-freeze in 'em." His hope was dashed. The liquid drained clear. It was pure water — meaning every machine must be drained.

Had he been his usual healthy vigorous self, it would have taken a quarter hour. In his weakened state, the la-borious task absorbed an hour, or more, during which his breath grew shorter. He was more chilled than ever. He became markedly shaky and questioned whether he could endure.

Somehow he finished. Every engine was drained of water. Thirty-two gallons poured from discharge valves and bled onto the darkened earth, where, by morning, it would freeze solid. The menacing threat to the Improvement Company was evaded; the peril to Levi Booth was not.

On unsteady legs, wheezing, coughing, and aching, he managed to re-enter the pickup and drive the return route to the Quarters. He pulled into the dirt driveway and switched off the motor. The front porch light was burning.

Cora dashed out, accompanied by her neighbor and closest friend, Adell Owens, a tall handsome woman whose skin was the color of mahogany. With their breaths exhaling frosty vapors, they found Levi behind the wheel, clutching it with both hands, rigid as a statue unable to move. After prying him out of the truck, and with one woman under each arm, they guided him into the house and onto a bed soon piled with blankets.

Staring at the ceiling, shivering and perspiring beneath the cover, he strained to speak in a weakened voice. Cora and Adell stood close to the bed. "No anti-freeze in any of 'em.... Had to drain 'em all.... Blocks won't bust now."

"I know it, Levi. God knows how I do know it. An' look at you. It's just what I was afraid of," replied Cora, as she turned and asked Adell to call Doctor James.

Neighbors drifted in and stood quietly against the bedroom wall. No greetings were exchanged when Doctor James entered, physician's bag in hand, and moved directly to Levi's bedside. Bespectacled, about sixty, gray hair, in manner and method he gave off confidence and experience. The white doctor leaned over the bed, removed the covers and examined the shaky, sweat-soaked black patient. His verdict came quickly. "This man must go to the hospital."

On the following Monday morning, the Improvement Company's Caterpillar operators reported for work. The weather was mild and clear. They put in a full day clearing land on the Bedford Tract.

Others were not as fortunate. As Levi predicted, the freakish freeze ruptured engine blocks and radiators across Hawkins County. Inoperable vehicles and machines began jamming garages and repair shops. Mechanics were soon working overtime. The whole economy was affected. In a front page story, the *Hawkins County Dispatch* stated: "It is impossible to calculate the damages."

Booth never came home from the hospital. The Death Certificate, signed by Doctor James on January 21, 1948, listed the cause of death as: "Viral pneumonia, aggravated by extreme exposure."

A week later the funeral filled the barn-like, high-steepled Beulah Baptist Church near the Quarters's main cross-road. Seated to the left of the main aisle, in a body, was Horace Howe and his entire family — wives, husbands, brothers, sisters, aunts, uncles, nephews, nieces. They filled five polished-wood pews, and all were aware of Levi Booth's good works. By their presence they were testifying to that which they did not — seemingly could not — articulate during Booth's lifetime, to wit: that he was commended, valued, appreciated; that the color of his skin, his ancestry, his class, the segregated order in which he lived were immaterial.

Horace Howe tried to speak. Upon a nod from the minister, he arose holding a single sheet of white paper with scribbling on it. He turned and faced the congregation, paused, looked up at the ceiling, down at the floor, and began, "Levi Booth... best man I ever knew... master mechanic... did many wonderful things for my company... loyal... resourceful..." There he stalled. The paper fluttered loose and drifted to the plank floor. Barely audible, he said, "I cannot speak any more."

Essays and Comments

A New Gilded Age

Beginning some three decades ago, America entered A New Gilded Age. To even the casual observer the evidence is everywhere. As with eras of the past, it has spawned a new breed of plutocrat. In the course of this paper, we will examine both.

The massive unprecedented bull market that began in 1983 and continuing until March 2000 generated phenomenal growth in the wealth of an already rich and powerful nation. During this period, the executive officer of the American corporation emerged to reap for himself and his own vast portions of the new riches. Are the interests of this new plutocrat and the public interest one and the same? Is there a hue and cry for reform? Is there a need for reform? If so, what kind of reforms are timely? Are they likely to come about?

There was, of course, a period of American life that Mark Twain labeled The Gilded Age. Its origins are traced to the 1870s and the explosion of invention, innovation, and industrial growth that followed the Civil War. It lasted for roughly half a century and was already in remission by the time of the 16th Amendment in 1913, authorizing imposition of a graduated income tax.

It was a period of incredible ostentation. Great limestone mansions rose in New York City. Even more stately pleasure domes were erected at Newport. Mrs. William K. Vanderbilt gave her $250,000 ball in 1893. That of Bradley Martin in 1897 was more lavish. For this the ballroom of the old Waldorf-Astoria was transformed into a replica of Versailles. One guest appeared in a suit of gold inlaid armor valued at $10,000. A little earlier at Del Monico's guests were given cigarettes wrapped in hundred dollar bills which they lighted with a legitimate sense of affluence.

Individual fortunes were of equal dimension. Between 1892 and 1899, Rockefeller's personal dividends from Standard Oil amounted to between $30,000,000 and $40,000,000. In 1900, Andrew Carnegie had an income from his steel companies of $23,000,000. These revenues were not subject to tax [and the dollar was then worth more than it is now]. In addition to oil, steel, railroads, real estate, copper, and banking other pursuits returned vast rewards. Some of this represented a return on capital. However, as the years passed much was related directly to strategic holds on what was then the sources of production—plants, mines, minerals, petroleum.

We associate the former age with the Vanderbilts, the Morgans, the Tweeds. We see it as major wealth concentrated in the hands of a few. We think of monopolies, trusts, cartels, and the manipulation of unregulated markets by powerful and avaricious men. We think of a demented era of American policies, when U.S. senators and state legislators were bought and sold by unfettered plutocrats, with their retinue of servants, mansions and art collections. The plutocrats were a force to be reckoned with, as they cut wide swaths in the economic and political life of American society.

The Gilded Age was marked by a wide "disparity in incomes and wealth" separating the rich from a middle class that was much smaller then than now. Poverty was rampant in this country. Beggars were found on the streets of the cities. Small wonder F. Scott Fitzgerald wrote "the rich are different from you and me." Indeed they were.

By and by America awakened. It occurred to the body politic that a market system, unregulated and left to the timeless forces of greed and avarice, resulted in trusts, monopolies, and cartels that abused, distorted, and suppressed competition. The trust busters burst on the national scene. Theodore Roosevelt was elected President The Sherman Anti-trust Act was passed, along with other landmark legislation. None was intended to strip the wealthy of their riches. The public policy behind the reforms was restoration of competition in the marketplace.

The reforms worked well until the crash of 1929 and the nation fell, stricken, in a Great Depression. It lay bare further abuses of the free market system, a further concentration of wealth, and the need for other reforms designed to restore integrity to the system, particularly in corporate finance and the securities market.

The country regained its confidence with the election of Franklin Roosevelt and the New Deal, World War II stimulated demand on American farmers and its factories. The war over, peacetime productions rose dramatically. Jobs were plentiful once more. Happy days were here again.

By the 1950s and 60s America had become largely a middle class society. The flagrant spectacles of the Gilded Age receded from public view. The Jekyl Island Club closed its doors. The vast wealth and income inequities diminished. Beggars and hobos disappeared from public view. Poverty was diminished. Movements in the business cycle were of mild consequence. The nation grew more prosperous than ever before.

By the 1980s a new economic epoch was underway. Paul Volcker and the Federal Reserve broke and defeated inflation. Interest rates began an historic decline. Unemployment fell below seven percent. Industrial production rose. The World Wide Web appeared on the scene—along with an unprecedented wave of technological innovations. Corporate profits soared, stimulating the greatest, longest bull market in Wall Street history. A New Gilded Age disclosed its own plutocrats.

Unlike the former Gilded Age, this one is unmarked by the founders and owners of oil refineries, banks, steel mills, and railroads. The plutocrats of our time are paid employees who haunt the corporate suites of public companies they rarely found or organize. They are the chief executive officers of those companies and corporations.

The New York Federal Reserve Bank reported that during the past twenty years the average CEO's compensation has grown from 42 times that of the average production worker to more than 400 times as much. That translates to an average CEO salary of $10,000,000 a year versus $25,467 for the average worker.

Over the past thirty years most people have seen only modest salary increases. The average annual salary in America, expressed in 1998 dollars (that is adjusted for inflation) rose from $32,520 in 1970 to $35,864 in 1999. That is about a 10 percent increase over 29 years—progress, but not a lot. Over the same period however, according to Fortune Magazine, the average real annual compensation of the top 100 CEOs went from $1,300,000—39 times the pay of an average worker—to $37,500,000, more than 1,000 times the pay of ordinary workers.

The explosion in CEO pay over the past thirty years is an amazing story in its own right and an important one. Let's look at some evidence. Scott McNely, CEO of troubled Sun Micorsystems, received a 2002 compensation package potentially valued at more than $87,000,000. He received stock options valued at $61,200,000 and exercised stock options for a $25,200,000 gain. Directors awarded him an additional option on 3,500.00 shares at exercise prices of $6.45 cents to $12.59. All this, said the board of directors, was intended to "directly motivate him to maximize stock holder value."

At beleaguered and bankrupt K-Mart, CEO James Adamson publically assumed full responsibility for his company's fate, vowing to do whatever he could to turn it around. While the retail chain was going down the tubes, however, the board of directors okayed tens of millions in bonuses and loans to Adamson and other top executives. The story has a familiar ring with Enron, Tyco, and other publically traded companies.

Boards of directors across the land have used super sized salaries, sweetheart loans, and generous stock options as a means of rushing to compensate top chief executives. For example, at World Com, the board of directors authorized a loan to CEO Bernie Ebbens of $406,000,000.

At Tyco International, the board of directors agreed to pay a severance package of $48,000,000 in cash to Mark H. Schwartz, its chief financial officer, while he himself was under investigation by a grand jury in Manhattan that later indicted him on fraud charges.

At Coca-Cola two and a half years ago, Dennis Ivester received a $90,000,000 severance package even while he was being discharged for inadequate performance.

Robert A. Daft of the Coca-Cola Company is receiving $67 million a year in compensation while the price of shares of his company have remained stagnant or declined for the last several years. Is any one employee worth $67,000,000?

Perks of the plutocrats are frequently hidden from view. But along comes a divorce proceeding of the legendary Jack Welch, Jr., of General Electric fame, and we get an inside view. His monthly living expenses alone are $366,114. He spends $5,480 a month on country club memberships; $13,258 a month on clothes, food, and drink; $425 on personal care and $1,480 on rental cars. He maintains two homes in Connecticut, two in Florida, and one in Nantucket, Massachusetts, the total monthly cost of which is $51,531. The estimated value of all of that real estate, plus a sixth property in Lennox, Massachusetts, is $30.7 million. It might be noted also that Mr. Welch's total personal assets of $456.2 million is half the gross domestic product of Monaco. The total GDP of Grenada, by comparison, is $394 million.

When Mr. Welch retired, he was granted for life the use of a Manhattan apartment including food, wine, and laundry, access to corporate jets, and a variety of other in-kind benefits worth $2 million a year. The perks illustrate the extent to which corporate leaders now expect to be treated like ancient regime royalty. In monetary terms, the perks must have meant little to Mr. Welch. In 2000, his last full year running G.E., he was paid $123 million, mainly in stock and stock options.

Ride around and look. Bob Nardelli, Home Depot CEO, and his wife paid $4.4 million for a two story stucco mansion in Buckhead in March 2001. They then hired an architect and proceeded to renovate the place. The heavily guarded and barely visible house is set about one hundred yards from the road, behind a stone wrought-iron fence, landscaped with large trees and scrubs. There is a compound of buildings which includes a free standing media house, a guest house, and pool with cabana attached to the garage. The garage attached to the house has three bays, and another garage to the rear has room for eight cars. Nardelli's home office is paneled in maple which reportedly cost $165,000. The total package is valued at $10 million. Thierry Despont is an Architect who specializes in houses for the super rich. He is known as the Eminence of Excess. He designs houses from 20,000 to 60,000 square feet and is doing a land-office business.

Opulence is everywhere. Armies of servants are back. Yachts are more in vogue than ever. And even J.P. Morgan did not own a Gulf Stream Jet. Dennis L. Kozlowski of Tyco International fame reported last year to the SEC that he spent $17,100 on an antique toilet kit, $15,000 on a poodle-shaped umbrella stand, and $5,560 on two sets of sheets.

Polly Onet, an event planner, whose clients include many established and aspiring corporate moguls, reports that weddings and birthdays run $150,000 to $3,000,000. She says, "You spend $200,000 on fireworks, $200,000 on renting a castle in Ireland, and then you take the guys out for a three day golf trip. It adds up. Just the floor in a tent can run you anywhere from $30,000 to $150,000.

And, yes, as in the past, The Gilded Age is marked by an income disparity. It has reached a point that the 13,000 richest families in America now have almost as much income as the 20 million poorest households. Those 13,000 families have incomes of 300 times that of average middle class families.

Surveys that track high incomes have found startling results. A recent study by the non-partisan Congressional Budget Office used income tax data and other sources to improvise on census estimates. The CBO study found that between 1979 and 1997 the after-tax income of the top one percent of families rose 157 percent, compared with only a ten percent gain for families near the middle of income distribution.

How have the relatively modest salaries of top corporate executives thirty years ago become the gigantic pay packages of today? A more optimistic story draws an analogy between that of CEO pay and the explosion of baseball salaries with the introduction with the free agency system.

One key reason is that executives are compensated by members of the very board of directors that they have a hand in appointing. It is not the invisible hand of the market that leads to those monumental executive incomes; it's the invisible handshake in the board room.

The increase in executive pay represents a social change, one that is more than a purely economic force of supply and demand. It is not a market trend like the rising value of waterfront property. It is more perhaps, like the sexual revolution of the 1960s—a relaxation of old strictures, a new permissiveness, In this case the permissiveness is financial.

Since the 1980s there has been evermore emphasis on the importance of "leadership," meaning personal, charismatic leadership. When Lee Iacocca became a business celebrity in the early 1980s, he was practically alone. In 1980, only one issue of Business Week featured a CEO on its cover. By 1999, the number was up to 19. Once it became normal, even necessary, for a CEO to be famous, it also apparently become easier to make him rich.

Another factor was the alignment of executive compensation with the rise in shareholder value. This mentality holds that is if the shareholder value rose, then the executive is entitled to share in that rise with executive stock options and the like. Jack Welch defended his rewards on grounds that General Electric shares rose substantially during his term.

In the 1980s and 90s business and the press collaborated in the creation of a mythical creature-the superstar CEO epitomized by Jack Welch. Superstar CEOs were deemed capable of revolutionizing companies with tens of thousands of employees. Boards of directors were so eager to reward there star executives that they agreed to let them continue feeding at the corporate trough even after they retired, for life in some instances. "The level of perks given CEOs should not come as a surprise" says Rakesh

Klaurama, Harvard Business Professor and author of *Searching for a Corporate Savior*. "The CEO, as charismatic leader, must be given all these things to prove his god-like powers, just like Shamans and there masks and amulets and the like."

Many will aver that the U.S. economic system may generate a lot of inequality. But it also generates much higher income than any alternative so that everyone is better off. That was the moral Business Week tried to convey in its (recent) special issue "25 Ideas for a Changing World." One of those ideas was "the rich get richer, and that's okay." High incomes at the top, the conventional wisdom declares, are the result of a free market system. If that provides a huge incentives for performance at the top that doesn't come at the expense of the rest of us.

Moreover, as the stock market rose to ever and ever greater heights during the 1980s and 90s the conventional wisdom held that whatever else you may say The Imperial CEO has delivered results that dwarfed the expense of executive compensation.

Bull markets do not last forever. The stock market bubble inevitably bursts. When it did it became alarmingly clear there was a price for those distorted pay packages. It was paid by the shareholders of the corporation.

The schemes designed to benefit corporate insiders to inflate the pay of the CEO and his inner circle were manifestations of one of man's oldest and most persistent urges - unmitigated greed. That is, they were all about "chaos of competitive avarice, often hidden and disguised by looting executives through complicated schemes of sweetheart loans, stock options, deferred compensation and the like." A view shared by Federal Reserve Chairman Alan Greenspan, who accused corporate executives of "infectious greed." It is evidenced by Dennis Kozolwski who pulled down $500,000,000 in pay during the half decade that he and his cronies are now accused of looting $600,000,000 from Tyco.

Those who pay the freight for executive compensation are the shareholders. It is they who capitalize the corporation through risks-capital investment. They are virtually powerless to do anything about executive compensation. This right and authority is vested in the board of directors and the compensation committees.

Scandals, breakdowns, collapses, and fraud at World Com, Tyco, Global Crossing, and others, coupled with the severe bear market on Wall Street have shaken confidence in the system. Executive compensation and the interests of shareholders became misaligned.

Board member John Bogle, widely respected in the securities community, and the founder of mutual fund giant Vanguard Group, said that stock options alone had "failed abjectly to do what they were ballyhooed to do, which was to align the management interest with those of shareholders."

The case for action was also made recently by New York Federal Reserve Bank President, William McDonough. He warned that ballooning executive compensation is jeopardizing public support for the USA's market system.

The Conference Board Commission of Public Trust and Private Enterprise is part of a wide-ranging corporate reform effort. It released its initial recommendations for dealing with the abuse and overall unfairness of American executive compensation practices. Proposals are pending that will give the Treasury and Internal Revenue Service new authority to restrict deferred-compensation plans. It includes a crack down on off-shore variations that analysts view as abusive. The measure pending in the House would end most, if not all, deferred compensation tax benefits altogether. One member of Congress noted that deferred compensation deals have allowed top executives to walk away from struggling or bankrupt companies with millions of dollars that are out of reach of creditors.

As executive pay draws more media and investor attention, the International Corporate Governance Network has come up with recommendations for remuneration packages. Some of these include:

- Disallowance of loans to executives from the corporation;
- Placing the costs of options in revenue accounts;
- Providing compensations in reports with accountability directly to shareholders published by every company;

- Remuneration committees composed of independent directors with final say;
- No transaction bonuses for takeovers or mergers;
- Full transparency of information.

This is after all the United States of America. The pursuit and accumulation of wealth are standing features of the culture. And I myself detect no rising tide that will result in complete reform, partial reform perhaps. It remains to be seen what the nation will do, if anything, concerning the rise and reign of its new Plutocrats.

For instance, much has been written and said about new accounting requirements; about compelling chief executives to sign off on public disclosures with the Securities and Exchange, and other adjustments to the status quo. But I for one, have heard no compelling oratory utterance from the president or his inner circle calling for radical change in executive compensation in this New Gilded Age.

Further I sayeth not.

American Life and Culture: A Random View

In this incidental survey of the scene, admittedly limited, I see more than one America. So let us begin with the first.

I see a great and mighty nation, as measured by the accepted method of economic strength, standards of living, and military capability. With collapse of the Soviet Union and end of the Cold War, now rapidly receding in mind and memory, the U.S. became, and remains, the one and only Super Power. The scale and dimensions of its power are unknown in the annals of history since the time of Octavious. Rising, yes, are China and its 1.4 billion mortals and India, with its teeming millions, 200 of which have no clean drinking water. America, however, at this point on the great arc of time and events, stands pre-imminent. Moreover, many people from across the globe want in.

Her military might is literally overwhelming. The armed forces number almost three million personnel, about half in reserve. In financing they are receiving $711 billion per year. That is nearly fifty percent of world military expenditures.

From all accounts, the armed forces are better trained, better equipped, and better able to carry out their missions than their predecessors. Their capacity to move personnel, equipment, and supplies from one end of the globe to the other, in large and small quantities, is astonishing to say the least. In addition, when called upon, it is lethal.

Who could forget the television interview of the two U.S. tankers who were veterans of the Gulf War? They related maneuvering their machines onto a rise in the sands of that god-forsaken desert and confronting a line of eleven Iraqi tanks arrayed against them. They described in detail, and to their own admitted disbelief, how they killed all eleven tanks without a scratch. Further they were astonished when the blasts of their cannons sent the turrets of the enemy tanks flying fifty feet in the air.

Consider the U.S. economy. Remember it is about half the size of Russia and three tenths the size of Africa—both of which are heavily endowed with natural resources. Yet, in 2008, the latest figures I could get, it is the largest in the world, at $14.2 trillion gross domestic product. GDP stands at $46,800 per capita. This is not the highest in the world. Actually, it ranks tenth, but who among you is unfortunate to have been born in this country.

Overall, the economic history of the U.S. is one of stable growth in GDP, a relatively low unemployment rate, and high levels of research, technological innovation, and capital investment, fueled by both national and foreign investors, the current recession notwithstanding. No other nation comes close to the efficiency of American agriculture, the land where the reaper was invented, hybrid corn was pollinated, and where the food store is a place of miracles—in terms of variety, quality, and availability of foodstuffs and consumables. The typical store carries 45,000 items!

Franklin Roosevelt declared, "The Trend of Civilization is upward." I submit America's political institutions have made a major contribution to that trend. We take it for granted they are divided—executive legislative judiciary—but this is an extraordinary arrangement among states and nations. In addition, we have a written constitution, one that lays out unassailable civil rights, in a manner unprecedented in the civilized world. Despots and tyrants do not ply their trade in this country. As Abraham Lincoln observed, "Other nations have come to power by depriving their people of rights, America rose by granting them."

This is the world's first large enduring republic. One that replaced divine rights, hereditary rights, customary legitimacy, and privilege, and placed supreme authority in its people, in the everyday, ordinary citizen. Make no mistake, and irrespective of the alleged anger emanating from certain conspicuous groups, the doors of opportunity are open to all, by operation of law.

Unique, extraordinary, beneficial to humankind—is that the American experience? I say the answer is an emphatic "yes."

In other ways its good deeds are manifest. It unshackled slavery, places a premium on fair play, defeated monopoly and restored competition in free markets. It helped stanch the bloodbath, the shambles and the shame that was World War I. It helped save western civilization in World War II. The Marshall Plan rebuilt a Europe starving, decimated, and cloaked in despair. Its humanitarian efforts, in natural disasters everywhere, are too numerous to name.

Concurrently I see another America, one characterized by accelerating change, economic crises, and dislocation. The scene is stuffed with thoughtless self-indulgence, consumption, and unchecked greed. Common are accounts of high-profile scandals, ethical fiascoes, non-stop, mass media-induced gullibility, a dumfounding lack of public accountability, and a ridiculous, so-called "war on drugs."

The country is afflicted with a pronounced bent toward excess. Americans extend and supersize everything. Coco-Cola sits on the shelf in quart bottles. You can buy a Snickers candy bar a foot long. The college football season is extended to twelve games. The professional football season is expected to lengthen another two games, from sixteen to eighteen. New homes now have screening rooms, and TV sets are available that are as large as the side of a house. In an age of lightning-fast communications, the tube, and jet airplanes—when one would think the opposite would be true—campaigns for public office grow longer and longer and longer and costlier and costlier and costlier.

We had a great ride. Beginning in the 1980s, and continuing pretty much unencumbered until 2008—irrespective of two wars on the other side of the globe—the economy grew, the job market expanded, the stock market created massive amounts of new wealth, and the word "billionaire" became part of the argot of the times. Interest rates were low, gas was cheap—relatively speaking—and the value of homes appreciated year after year after year, to the point homeowners were re-financing to claim abundant equities. Lenders concluded the price of an American residence would appreciate in perpetuity. From 1980 to 2007, the median price of a new home quadrupled. The Dow Jones Industrial Average climbed from 803 in the summer of 1982 to 14,165 in the fall of 2007.

An excess of wealth became evident throughout the country. Office building lobbies went marble. Limos multiplied. McMansions sprouted in subdivisions and suburbs. Kobe beef steaks became available in various joints for $175.00, and three cars for every family became the norm. Vast auto parking lots on college campuses filled with student-driven SUVs. Last year, according to Time magazine, thirty managers of the top hedge funds received compensation totaling $11.5 billion. By the way, you can now purchase a special ticket to a Yankee baseball game for $325. It includes an all-you-can-eat buffet. The Spotted Pig, a fancy Manhattan gastro-pub, provides the grub.

We have become a nation of gamblers. Until the late '80s, only Nevada and New Jersey had casinos. Now twelve states do and forty-eight have some form of legalized betting. Better to gamble than save. Back in 1982, the average household saved 11 percent of its disposable income. By 2007, that number was less than 1 percent. State lotteries are acceptable across the nation.

Obesity surges unchecked. During the period of the long run, the average American gained about a pound a year, so that an adult of a given age is now at least 20 pounds heavier than someone the same age back then. In the late '70s, 15 percent of Americans were obese. Today, a third of the citizenry are. Everywhere I turn in Dublin, and elsewhere, I see overweight young people, often with bloated children in tow. Compare that to South Korea where the obesity rate is 3.5 percent of the population. One morning last week, while at the coffee group that meets at a McDonald's restaurant, I watched as a young woman, who could not have been over twenty, eating a large hamburger and french fries for breakfast. Across the table was a small child, not more than 6 or 7, and greatly over weight, eating the same things.

Food is everywhere. Suburbs are ringed with restaurants. Fast food and chain eateries dot strip malls and roadways. Social functions offer vast spreads. In addition, we have already noted the varities of the food store.

Thanks largely to the availability of nitrogen-based fertilizers, effective pesticides, and the American farmer's competence in food production. Since 1945, the food supply has increased faster than the population—and as George Will notes, "...faster even than Americans can increase their feasting."

And Americans are paying the price. According to Michael Pollan, author of *The Omnivore's Delight*, when you adjust for age rates of chronic disease like cancer and ype 2 diabetes are considerably higher today than they were in 1900. Will also points out that type 2 diabetes was called adult-onset diabetes until children starting getting it. Now it is a $100 billion a year consequence of among other things, obesity related to a diet of corn-fed steaks and chops that have pushed plants off the plate. Meanwhile, The Nation's Food Bank Network estimates Americans waste nearly 96 billion pounds of food each year.

The nation has a massive eating disorder. They eat in moving vehicles, for heaven's sake. Americans reportedly eat one of five meals in motor vehicles. The typical gas station makes more money from food and cigarettes than from the sale of fuel. One of three children eats fast food every day.

John Lukas, author of the book, *The Last Rites*, reports a poll was taken of children in a New Jersey grammar school. Three of 45 had a sit-down meal at home each day. What does this say about society, about the kind of people we have become?

Meanwhile as Americans gorge themselves, experts at the UN food and aid organization estimate 1 billion people are hungry on the this planet of misfortune. The recent economic downturn is expected to increase that number by 104 million.

The land of the free and home of the brave? Yes, and the domicile of the prison inmate. The prison population has skyrocketed over the past quarter century. In 1982, 1 in 77 adults were in the correctional system, in one form or another, totaling 2.2 million people.

In 2007 a record number of Americans served time in the corrections system. The U.S. corrections population—those in jail, prison, on probation or parole—totaled 7.3 million, or 1 in every 31 adults. Blacks are four times more likely than whites to be in corrections systems, according to the Pew Center on States, an information gathering entity. The U.S. has 5 percent of the world's population, but 25 percent of the world's prison inmates.

This mess has resulted largely from state policy choices that have placed ever-longer sentences on many low level offenses, drug violations in particular. In fact and reality, the jails are full of drug offenders; the cities are full of drug related criminality, and trafficking thrives in prohibited substances and firearms.

Based on estimates from the White House Office of National Drug Control Policy, Americans spend $64 billion a year on illegal drugs. And according to a 2006 study by the former president of the National Organization for the Reform of Marijuana Laws Jon Gettman, marijuana is already the top cash crop in 39 states, with a total annual value of $36 billion. These sordid transactions are off the books—state and federal governments receive no tax revenue from this monumental industry. What duty should rest upon one private citizen to prevent another from smoking a joint? Is the drug problem a health problem, or a problem of criminality? Why a war on our fellow citizens?

Last November before dawn at a Wal-Mart in Valley Stream, New York, crazed shoppers, lured by cheap consumer electronics and discounted toys, trampled to death a fellow shopper, all attempting to enter the place. The incident gained national attention, as it should, but it also lays bare a pervasive addiction to consumption, rising to the level of a national sickness. Fueled by television advertising and the availability of plastic card credit, Americans have been on a buying binge for decades. In unbelievable quantities, they have purchased appliances, toys, clothes, gadgets, and junk. Writing in Newsweek, Anna Quindlen, says that by 2010 Americans will be a trillion dollars in the hole on credit-card debt alone.

An entire industry of off-premises storage has emerged just to store much of the stuff. If not in a bin then in some cavernous house with a garage big enough to start a homeless shelter.

My younger brother is in the process of moving from his home in Atlanta back to a farm home in Wayne

County. He told me recently, "I cannot believe the amount of stuff we have bought and put in this house." He does not know it, but I once looked where he stores his hunting gear. The place held enough camouflage clothing to outfit a platoon of hunters

The satirical newspaper, The Onion, published a piece in June 2005, originating—it claimed—from Fenghua, China. It quotes one Chen Hsien, an employee of Fenghua Ningbo Plastic Works Ltd., a plastic factory that manufactures lightweight household item for Western markets. Says Chen:

> I can hardly believe the sheer amount of garbage Americans will buy. Often, when we're assigned a new order for say 'salad shooters,' I will say to myself, 'There's no way that anyone will ever buy these.' ... One month later, we will receive an order for the same product, but three times the quantity for the same product. How can anyone have a need for such useless garbage? I hear that Americans can buy anything they want, and I believe it, judging from the things I've made for them."
> He adds: "And I also hear that, when they no longer want an item they simply throw it away. So wasteful. So contemptible.

Writing in *The New York Times*, columnist Tom Friedman states:

> We have created a system for growth that depends on our building more and more stores, to sell more and more stuff, made in more and more factories in China, powered by more and more coal that would cause more and more climate change, but to earn China more and more dollars to buy more and more U.S. T-bills so America would have more and more money to build more and more stores and buy more and more stuff that would employ more and more Chinese."
>
> If stuff is not salvation, why in the world do we buy all this junk? Is there any meaning to it? If the house were burning down, it is unlikely one would grab first a souped-up microwave from Target. Yet the entire economy appears to rise and fall from consumer spending. President Bush exhorted the citizenry to "go shopping."

Consumption is not limited to gadgets and minor personality. A car for the sixteen-year-old has become a rite of passage. Schools must arrange parking space for student vehicles, meanwhile the bus is half empty and mom is waiting in line in a string of vehicles to pick up Johnny, or drop him off in the morning. In Ocilla, Georgia, population about 2,500, a home under renovation will have an eight-car garage. The American household is equipped with conveniences and comforts unimaginable to the potentate of yesteryear, or even U.S. citizens of the last generation.

And speaking of homes and houses, all one has to do is look around at these huge, magnificent, beautifully equipped and furnished places and wonder how people afford them. A local banker once observed that younger people buying new homes during the bubble never expected to pay for them. A complete turn-around from a generation ago, when paying for one's home was a priority and a personal achievement.

A word or two about the tube and World Wide Web, and I shall limit it to a word or two. Much of technology is far beyond me and, to be sure, the scope of this paper, but consider this. Prevention magazine reports in its June issue that the average American spends 151 hours per month watching TV. The number of hours per month of TV watching associated with a 23 percent rise in obesity is 60. The number of hours per month of TV watching associated with a 14 percent rise in the risk of diabetes is 60. The maximum number of hours per month of TV watching recommended for ideal health is 30.

As for the Web, no one can deny it is everything at once. If not already, it is rapidly becoming the primary medium for communication and information and a place to go to shop, play, debate, and find love. Lee Siegel, in his new book, *Man Against the Machine*, contends we cede more and more control of freedom and individuality to the needs of the machine and technology, whose boundaries stretch to encompass human activity across the spectrum. Supposedly, we are living in the golden age of information, where anyone can find any name, any date, any historical detail, any formula with a click of the mouse.

It's for certain, a generation of children, to a marked degree, have fled the out of doors and school playgrounds stripped of equipment, to glue themselves to the TV screen for games and the internet. And study after study has revealed that the attention span of old and young across the board has shortened. Newspapers are in decline. The language is corrupted.

Along with the war on drugs, the war on sex has also failed. Teenagers continue to have children; a phenomenon no one believes is healthy for the mother, the child, for society. This despite the fact Congress has poured $1.5 billion into what is essentially anti-sex education and abstinence-only programs. A study conducted by the Department of Health and Human Services during the Bush administration, showed that teenagers enrolled in abstinence-only programs were just as likely to have sex as those who didn't. Texas, for instance, leads the nation in spending for abstinence-only programs. Meanwhile it has one of the highest teen pregnancy rates in the country.

Is criminality, obesity, crime, consumption, and materialism indicative of decadence and a downward spiral and decline? Are we the self-inflicted victims of a painful contagious socially transmitted condition of overload and waste, resulting from the dogged pursuit of more? Can we go on living large? Or, are we simply marking footprints on the sands of time? When all is said and done, does it really matter a damn?

These questions are beyond the scope of this paper and surely the wisdom of the writer. I do suspect, however, that the trends, impulses, and vagaries of the times call into question that everlasting American axiom, to wit: *growth, progress, and prosperity are inevitable; our children will have it better than we did.*

Conflict and Politics: The Early Years

From the Doublin Courier Herald, May 20, 2008

This piece will address political sentiments that permeated American public life during the early years. Emphasis will fall upon individuals, issues, factions, and parties, such as they were. The time frame begins with Colonial America in the year 1763. It trails off with the presidential elections of Andrew Jackson in 1828 and Abraham Lincoln in 1860. It's an old story, one with which many are familiar—to greater or lesser degrees.

Nevertheless, even in these times of incessant electioneering something may be gained. A citizen, a voter, somewhere, might benefit from raising once more history's curtain and peering at the stew from which sprang "…a nation conceived in liberty and dedicated to the proposition that all men are created equal." After all, said Aristotle, "Man is a political creature." And Walt Whitman added, "For what is the present but a growth out of the past?"

Yes! There was once in this country a violent political revolution. Voices grew shrill. Radical factions formed. A bloody armed conflict ensued. Victory at the end transferred power and property and established the American idea. It was an extremist thing. The dangers and difficulties were monstrous. One can lose one's head in revolutions. "If you smite at the King," said Machiavelli, "you better kill him."

Revolutions demand profound convictions, unimpeachable integrity, and unwavering courage. Political skills, a capacity to sprout and spread propaganda, a willingness to employ firearms and weapons, were all attributes of the revolutionary, in the eighteenth-century. Very few possessed them.

It is astonishing that rustic, thinly-populated Colonial America could produce an entire band of these stalwart souls. During the period in question, most of its inhabitants were poorly educated, if at all. They were struggling to survive in a still-primitive land. And there weren't many of them. The total population was barely three million, of which 250,000 were black slaves. Half the people in Virginia were in slavery. In South Carolina two-thirds of the population were slaves.

Life was hard in Colonial America. Everyday living absorbed time and energy. Misery and poverty abounded.

People got sick and died with great regularity. As late as 1900, life expectancy in America was 49 years. God knows what it was in 1763, or 1793.

The Colonists were strung out along the edge of the eastern seaboard. Communication—the mother's milk of politics and revolutions—was by stagecoach, horseback, sailing vessel, and the human foot. Time requirements were measured in weeks, sometimes in months. Schools were virtually non-existent, outside Philadelphia, New York, and Boston. Books were scarce. For many citizens, the only written word was *The Holy Bible*.

Soon after he became president in 1789, George Washington made a tour of the country. He was appalled at conditions of roads, bridges, and housing from one end of the country to the other. It is doubtful the same conditions in 1763 were any better. And, of course, the colonists were subjects of the laws of England and the edicts of King George III. At one period of his life, the man went insane but regained his wits by time of the Revolution. His mental illness is beautifully portrayed in the superb film, *The Madness of King George*.

From the colonial *hoi polloi*, emerged a collection of educated, widely read political geniuses and outright radicals. Many were steeped in the writings of the period's prominent philosophers of government and politics, statecraft, if you will: mainly John Locke of England and Montesquieu of France. Among them were Alexander Hamilton, Thomas Jefferson, John Adams, Sam Adams,

Patrick Henry, James Madison, John Jay, and George Mason. They enjoyed essential support of the Honorable George Washington and, perhaps the wisest of the lot, Benjamin Franklin. These distinguished men would provide leadership in the coming American Revolution and later at the Constitutional Convention of 1787.

Preceding both episodes was a span of grass-roots politics. Beginning about 1763, an attitude began to spread slowly favoring freedom from government authority, detachment from the bonds of Britain, and the achievement and preservation of "liberty," a shock word of the times. As one writer puts it, "First was the question of home rule, the second that of who should rule at home."

Thus, the first consequential political issue was the question of separation from the mother country. Up from the ooze arose two factions, to wit: Radicals and Republicans. The Radicals {who, as time passed, would include many of the founding fathers} began to agitate for a free and independent America, totally shed of what they called "English tyranny." The more conservative Republicans espoused maintenance of some British connections. Neither Radicals nor Republications formed political parties as such, defined by Edmund Burke of the British Parliament as "...a body united for promoting by their joint endeavors the national interest upon some particular principle upon which all are in agreement."

The issue of separation dug deep, and it had staying power. American politics swirled around it for years; *even after* the First Continental Congress convened in 1774; *even after* the outbreak of hostilities at Lexington and Concord in April 1775; *even after* Washington took the field later that year with the rag-tag Continental Army. Many Colonists believed the Revolutionary War was about redress of British grievances rather than total independence.

Often overlooked is the degree to which the colonies had achieved self-rule. Before the Revolution, practically all claimed some form of self government with substantial powers and authority. Membership in colonial governing bodies was composed of professional people, planters, land owners, and wealthy merchants—without exception. They were the forum for much political debate, but not all. Correspondence, pamphlets, and newspapers were also influential.

It was 1763 that marked a turning point. Until then, as Benjamin Franklin put it, the temper of America towards Great Britain was, "The best in the world." Thereafter, public opinion began its shift sanctioning the idea of independence. The movement gathered momentum year by year as Parliament passed The Stamp Act, The Quartering Act {requiring the colonies to provide free supplies for English troops stationed in Colonial Barracks}, and The Townsend Act {imposing duties on glass, lead, paper, and tea}. The importation of German soldiers to fill British ranks was especially repugnant.

Parliament's actions incited the body politic. They roused Sam Adams and the Radicals to host a famous "tea party" in Boston harbor. On the night of December 16,

1773, 300 spectators watched from the harbor wharves as white men, masquerading as Mohawks, boarded ships and hurled tea chests into the salt waters.

Britain began imposing the distasteful laws for a reason. The colonies had matured economically, to the degree that England became increasingly dependent upon them for commerce, trade, and tax revenue. A fleet of packet ships sailing back and forth between the two countries hastened the flow. Moreover, England's wars in Europe left her facing a large war debt, a further inducement to raise revenue from across the Atlantic.

Subordination of the colonies to British rule was an accepted proposition of all English statesmen. Meanwhile, the colonies' growing power of self-rule fermented less responsiveness to British demands. Still, objection to total independence stood steady as late as the winter of 1776, with a war in progress and the Second Continental Congress divided between Radicals and Conservatives, though Radicals held the upper hand.

Public opinion took a quantum leap for independence in January 1776, with publication of the booklet *Common Sense*. Its author was Thomas Paine, an Englishman, who immigrated only fourteen months prior to publication. The work found an immediate audience and approving readers. Sam Adams and his radical compatriots had discovered a writer sympathetic to the rebel cause, one with a first-rate pen who could state persuasively the case for American independence.

Mentioned earlier was a revolution's potential need for propaganda. Paine proved the propagandist *par excellence*. Even in those backward times of slow communications, the booklet spread rapidly and electrified the citizenry. George Trvelyn wrote in his *History of the American Revolution*, as follows:

> It would be difficult to name any human composition which has had an effect at once so insistent, so extended and so lasting...It worked nothing short of political miracles and turned Tories into Whigs

Another wrote:

> Paine brings to the burning issues of Philadelphia in 1776 the theoretical basis for the American Revolution and independence of the colonies.

The booklet went through fifty-six printings in 1776. One of Paine's biographers estimated 500,000 copies were printed that year alone. Here are a few excerpts:

> Society in every state is a blessing, but government, even in its best state is but a necessary evil; in its worst state, an intolerable one.

When we are planning for posterity, we ought
to remember that virtue is not hereditary.
Ye that love mankind, ye that dare oppose
not only tyranny but the tyrant, stand forth.

Spurred by sweeping change in public opinion, the Continental Congress {which the British considered an illegal body} resolved to issue a statement of intentions. It appointed Jefferson, Franklin, and John Adams on a committee to draw one. With some assistance, but very little, Jefferson composed the first draft. It underwent few changes, either by the committee or the Congress. Words condemning the British people and the slave trade were stricken, albeit Jefferson was a slave owner, some with very light skins.

The document was then published as the Declaration of Independence on or about July 4, 1776. Though widely circulated, it took time for it to become recognized for what it was—a foundation instrument of American government. Abraham Lincoln made major use of it throughout his political career, including issuance of the 1862 Emancipation Proclamation. Jefferson's words are unforgettable:

> When in the course of human events, it becomes necessary for one people to dissolve
> the political bands which have connected
> them with another, and to assume among

the powers of the earth, the separate and
equal station to which the Laws of Nature
and of Nature's God entitle them, A decent
respect to the opinions of mankind requires
that they should declare the causes which
impel them to the separation.
We hold these truths to be self evident, that
all men are created equal, that they are endowed by their Creator with certain un-
alienable rights, that among these are life,
liberty, and the pursuit of happiness.

Who could forget the television footage from city streets,
somewhere in Poland, during its revolt with the Soviet
Union? A mechanic in grease-stained clothing stood atop
a parked car surrounded by a swarm of listeners. He was
reading a fluttering copy of the Declaration, even as
strong winds threatened to tear it from his hands.

The issue of absolute independence continued burning throughout the Revolutionary period. Those in Congress supporting ties with Britain were part of a loose
contingent known as "Tories," or as they preferred, "Loy-
alists." They were in the minority but refused to cross the
line. The opposition was known as "Patriots." Even they
were unable to muster an absolute consensus.

The founders gravitated toward the Patriots. George
Washington, himself, favored total independence, though
the war's final outcome was doubtful. As the richest man

in America he stood to lose more than anyone, both his head and his fortune. On August 27, 1776, before the Battle of Long Island, Washington addressed the Continental Army. He declared:

> The time is now at hand which must probably determine whether Americans are to be free men or slaves. The fate of unborn millions will now depend, under God, on the courage and conduct of the army…We have, therefore, to resolve to conquer or to die.

With cessation of the Revolutionary War at Yorktown on October 17, 1781, the issue of independence was resolved conclusively and relegated to history. Victory in the long struggle was largely due to the character, diligence, and resolve of the one indispensable man in the entire episode, General George Washington. His career is a standing monument to the principle that in public life wisdom is of greater value than brilliance.

The Revolutionary War left a lasting residue. It sealed in the American mentality a perpetual set of values and beliefs, to wit: individual freedom and liberty, government only with consent of the governed, no taxation without representation, free elections and democracy, the equality of man, the contractual nature of government.

From abstract thought political institutions do not spring fully grown. They evolve with time and experience.

Difficulties encountered by Washington, his staff, and the Continental Congress in maintaining a land army through thirteen independent states and a weak central government left a profound impression. In particular the experience burned itself into the fertile minds of Alexander Hamilton and John Adams.

When peace returned it soon became apparent the central government's 1781 Articles of Confederation were inadequate. They proved unresponsive in matters of national defense and in regulation of commerce among the several states. As a result the second great political question of the times presented itself, to wit: *Must we have some kind of stronger central government? And if so, what form should it take?*

Again political factions arose. On the one hand were those who sought a federal government with powers. Among its leaders were, John Adams, John Jay, James Madison, and, of course, the ubiquitous Hamilton. Jefferson led the opposition. As it turned out, he held a mistaken view of the country's future course. He foresaw a nation dominated by independent yeoman farmers. He and his fellow travelers leaned toward individual freedom and limited government. Hamilton and his believers perceived an America of industry, commerce, and investment. Proponents would debate these contentions when the Constitutional Convention convened at Independence Hall in 1787.

The Convention, itself, became a reality following extensive agitation and volumes of correspondence. Significant, too, was a 1785 meeting at Alexandria, Virginia. Representatives from Maryland and Virginia requested it to discuss problems with navigation on the Potomac River. While the meeting was in progress, George Washington gave a dinner for the attendees at Mount Vernon. Over sherry and fine food, the guests concluded problems confronting their two states were common across the country. From this obscure meeting, a two-year quest began for a national assemblage to form a different kind of central government. By late spring 1787, delegates elected by the states began arriving in Philadelphia.

About the convention. First, Washington presided but rarely spoke. Second, delegates came and went. Of the total of seventy-four, only forty were present at any one time. Third, Congress instructed the delegates to begin their work in May. However, it was August before the last of them trickled in and final work began. Fourth, sessions were conducted behind closed doors. Each delegate was sworn to secrecy. Madison alone was authorized to take notes. They are an original source from which historians and constitutional scholars have reconstructed proceedings of the gifted politicians there assembled.

James Madison is often called "the Father of the Constitution" and for good reason. Long before delegates arrived in Philadelphia, he composed the complete draft of a constitution. It proved an invaluable working document, and most of it was left intact. Sections were rewritten only after the convention reached certain key compromises. Madison, incidentally, was 36 when business began.

Jefferson was not present in Philadelphia. He and John Adams were in France and England on diplomatic missions. Though a convention promoter and advocate of a strong federal government, Hamilton was often absent. When present he spoke eloquently for a potent new order at the national level. Also absent were Patrick Henry and Sam Adams.

No doubt existed as to the convention's mission. It was to form a new government, and it did. The delegates themselves came from some of the most prominent men in each state. Most were college graduates, a remarkable fact for that day and time. Lawyers predominated. No member of the small farmer and laboring classes was present. Political scientist Thomas J. Askew of the University of Georgia described the delegate body as follows:

> The delegates were on the whole, men of high principles. The elimination of the political and economic chaos then existing and establishment of national integrity through a strong central government far exceeded in importance in their minds any desire for personal gain.

Among those in attendance, not previously identified, were Edmund Randolph of Virginia, James Wilson and

Gouverneur Morris of Pennsylvania, Eldridge Gerry and Rufus King of Massachusetts, Roger Sherman and Oliver Ellsworth of Connecticut, William Livingston and William Paterson of New Jersey, Charles Pinckney of South Carolina, and Abraham Baldwin of Georgia. The other delegate from Georgia was William Few. One of his direct descendents was a beautiful co-ed at Emory University in the 1960s. Her name was Carol Few.

The political geniuses assembled at Philadelphia fulfilled their charge. They produced a written constitution, one that would withstand time and the eternal, impregnable constant of social and economic change. For some delegates the document was stronger than wanted. For others it was weaker. Madison would later say: "Every word of the new constitution decides a question between power and liberty." As originally adopted it consisted of a Preamble and seven short Articles containing all told about 4,000 words. The Preamble set forth its purposes. It states:

> We the people of the United States, in order to form a more perfect union, establish justice, insure domestic tranquility, provide for the common defense, promote the general welfare, and secure the blessings of liberty to ourselves and our posterity, do ordain and establish this constitution for the United States of America.

In its many opinions, the Supreme Court has frequently referenced words in the Preamble.

Article VII required ratification by nine of the thirteen states. Congress received it on September 20, 1787 and submitted it to the states without comment. By June 21, 1788, the necessary nine had ratified. The big states of New York and Virginia were yet to vote.

The clash on ratification was the dominant issue of the day. Political lines were tightly drawn. The Federalists urged ratification, though many of that persuasion believed the document created a government lacking sufficient power. The Anti- Federalists opposed on various grounds. The Federalists were the wealthy, creditors, and the merchant classes. The Anti-Federalists were laborers, debtors, and Jefferson's esteemed small farmers. Cities with large seaports leaned toward ratification.

Ratification lured the indefatigable Hamilton. He, along with Madison and John Jay, collaborated to write and publish eighty-five essays that became known as the *Federalist Papers*. These writings approved ratification and contained broad-ranging comment on the federal government. They became an important factor in the ratification process. The Papers are regarded, to the present day, as authoritative expositions on the constitution's meaning and effect.

At the New York ratification convention, where approval wavered, Hamilton brought to bear all political skills. John Jay assisted, and the measure passed in a close vote of 30 to 27. Henry Cabot Lodge, himself a veteran of thirty-seven years of service in one legal body or another, said of Hamilton's efforts, "He rendered pre-eminent service to the adoption of the Constitution. Tried by the severest test, that of winning votes. Hamilton's victory was of the highest rank."

In Virginia the influence of Washington, Madison, John Marshall, and Edmund Randolph brought success in another close vote of 89 to 79. Among delegates to ratification conventions held in each state, 843 voted "yes" and 476 voted "no."

The main objection Anti-Federalists raised to ratification was the document contained no protection of basic freedoms. The Federalists assured the people that if ratified the constitution would be amended to add them. Once more the talented Madison turned to. He drew up a set of seventeen amendments, some of which were suggested by Jefferson {among his was the right to trial by jury}. They were introduced in the new Congress and then in the several states. In 1791 ten were adopted and became known as "The Bill of Rights." They guarantee the rights of free speech, freedom of the press, the right to bear arms and so on. As time passed the amendments have become pivotal parts of the constitution and the subject matter of landmark Supreme Court cases. Madison's role in passage of the bill of rights was but one of many achievements. The diminutive Virginian had become a figure of national reputation.

America's second great political issue was resolved. The former colonies were now states, united by a single federal government created by compact. Rights not contained in the constitution were left to the residuary powers of the states; nor could a popular majority quash or abridge the document's guaranteed rights. On its path to becoming a nation of laws and not of men, America had crossed another threshold. Its fundamental, organic law was now embodied in a binding instrument adopted and ratified by the people.

By the late eighteenth-century slavery had become entrenched in the nation's economic life. More than one convention delegate owned plantations and held in bondage men whose skins were black. It is no mystery, therefore, they steered clear of one item that would later rise to haunt the nation—the institution of slavery; even though abolitionists were already becoming active in New England. Instead the delegates adopted the three-fifth compromise. It provided that in ascertaining the population for purposes of apportioning representation and direct taxes, three-fifths of the slave population would be counted.

The convention also implemented a provision that restrictions on the slave trade were prohibited prior to the year 1808. The word "slave" does not appear in the constitution. They fell under the category of "such persons." Bear in mind this was years *before* Whitney invented the gin and let loose America's first great economic tide, but *after* the Declaration declared "All men are created equal."

The constitution having become the law of the land, George Washington was elected without opposition as first president of the United States. He was inaugurated April 30, 1789. Alexander Hamilton was named secretary of the treasury, Thomas Jefferson secretary of state, and Edmund Randolph became attorney general. Despite his isolation at Monticello during the Revolutionary War, Jefferson had surfaced as a national political figure, one with a strong following and diplomatic experience. The first government, therefore, was comprised of founders all, save Henry Knox, secretary of war.

From the time of Washington and Jefferson down to date, the fundamental question underlying American politics was and is, "What should the government do?" Or stated differently, "What action should the government take?" Candidates for public office may not openly admit it, but their objective is to take control of the government through legal means and do with it as they wish. Ever heard a campaigning candidate declare, "We're going to take it [the government] back"? The same frame of mind is the driving motivation for organization and perpetuation of political parties.

The first president served two full terms but refused a third in 1796. Washington's steady hand and unimpeachable judgment proved of great advantage. By this time he had become practically a cult figure. No one said "no" to the man throughout his first term. He considered the new constitution an experiment in self government. He refused excess power and wisely led his administration in a manner that established and strengthened the new republic. Despite his great prudence, however, the president failed to foresee the rise or value of political parties. He denounced their inevitable emergence in what he called "The National Government." In a democracy, however, parties are predestined, as citizens of like political beliefs aggregate to impose their agenda upon governmental power.

Ironically, it was to Washington's administration that parties of the time traced their disorganized beginnings. Secretary of the Treasury Hamilton and Secretary of State Jefferson held opposing views of politics, of society, and of direction the new government should take. Their followers settled into adverse coalitions, more so than formal parties with organizational structure.

Before examining the Hamilton-Jefferson cleavage, a digression is in order. It concerns an incident in Congress that carried ominous implications. On February 11, 1790, two Quaker delegations—one from New York, one from Pennsylvania—not one of whom fired a shot in the Revolutionary War, presented petitions to the House. They sought an immediate end of the slave trade.

Congressional leaders instantly recognized the explosive potential, notwithstanding the constitution prohibited restrictions prior to 1808. They concluded contentions surrounding slavery could shatter the fledgling government. James Jackson of Georgia asked, "What standing could such dedicated pacifists enjoy among veterans of the revolution, who risked their lives and fortunes to secure for the community their liberty and property?" Others saw the move as a stalking horse for a scheme to end slavery, altogether. Abraham Baldwin of Georgia believed that any attempt to negotiate the slavery issue at the Constitutional Convention would have provoked its adjournment and killed the federal government at the moment of its birth.

Again, James Madison became congressman of the hour. He instigated a plan that allowed public debate on the issue but assured its death in committee. For the first time in American politics slavery was debated in public. Words were spoken that would not be repeated until advent of the Civil War. Just as Madison planned, however, following debate the petitions were shelved. The issues raised lay dormant for decades. Public Issue Number One became government finances.

These were Alexander Hamilton's politics, and they brought his greatness to full flower. He had shown an interest in business and commerce going back to his youth, when at age 15 he was put in charge of the West Indies trading company of Beckman and Kruger. Friends, and a few distant relatives, saw promise in the precocious lad with no father. They raised money for his passage to New York and enrollment in King's College, later Columbia University. He never returned to the Indies, became intensely patriotic, and joined the continental army, where he served as a trusted member of Washington's staff. Later in the war he commanded troops on the battlefield.

Of all the great citizens, Hamilton displayed superior talent at an earlier age than any, his commander-in-chief excepted. No American lawyer has ever risen higher from more humble beginnings, save Abraham Lincoln.

As to funding the federal government, Hamilton convinced President Washington that if it were going to accept the power it must assume fiscal responsibility. The Secretary promptly began guiding the nation's economy through establishment and enforcement of a system of taxation, to the extent Washington used federal troops to put down the Whiskey Rebellion in western Pennsylvania. This horrified Jefferson and his believers. They flinched at the exercise of governmental power in almost any form.

Hamilton's policies were continuing. He funded the national debt and restored the country's credit worthiness. He persuaded Congress to set up a mint and create a safe currency. He proposed a national bank. Foreseeing that commerce and industry would eventually dominate the economy, he fought for and won tariff protection for industry. He put in place a national debt so the country could finance needed infrastructure. In a forty-page *Report on the Public Credit*, he calculated the public debt at the daunting sum for that day of $77.1 million. Of that amount $11.7 million was owed to foreign governments; $40.4 million was domestic debt, most of which dated from the war; $25 million was state debt, also largely a war legacy.

A key feature of Hamilton's program was the federal government's assumption of state debt. Strangely enough,

Madison opposed the measure and became leader of the opposition. He argued the issue was about the hated enemy—power from on high. Hamilton's plan, as Madison saw it, concentrated too much power in the federal government. This historic disagreement ingrained American politics with an everlasting source of bedrock bile, to wit: *What action should the government take, or not take, and to what extent?*

Once Hamilton encountered a major hurdle, he launched into the offensive, acted decisively, and invited stragglers and the uncommitted to step aside. He was bold and aggressive. His mental energies were formidable. Whereas, both Madison and Jefferson were of a non-combative temperaments. They maneuvered by stealth and softer technique.

On Sunday, June 10, 1790, Jefferson hosted a famous dinner at which Madison and Hamilton were invited guests. Jefferson's idea was to bring the antagonists together in hopes a compromise would follow. The main point of contention was the federal government's assumption of state debt. An ancillary issue revolved around location for a new national capitol. When Washington was inaugurated in 1789, the capitol was in New York. The following year it was moved to Philadelphia. Construction of the new capitol began in 1797. He was the only President who did not live in Washington D.C.

Jefferson's dinner *did* lead to a settlement, one that approved most of Hamilton's proposals. The compromise included an agreement to build the national capitol on the Potomac River and to procure an accounting prior to assumption of state debt. When put into effect the secretary of the treasury's financial plan had the beneficial effects he anticipated. Public credit was hastily restored. Government bonds were soon selling at home and abroad at prices even or above par value. *Fortune Magazine* once published a lengthy article on all former secretaries of the treasury. It ranked Hamilton first and foremost—by a wide margin.

Debate on Hamilton's programs arose early in Washington's first administration. As expected, the president stamped them with approval. Public finance brought on the opening eruption between Jefferson and Madison, on the one hand, and Hamilton on the other. The fissure led to the rough amalgamation of two splinter groups. Hamilton's followers were known as "Federalists." The Jeffersonian contingent was called "Republicans."

The constitution makes no provisions for political parties. Even Washington's outspoken opposition did not deter the political combatants. The Federalists sought order and stability. Jefferson wrote and spoke of the primary importance of individual freedom and greatness of the nation's yeoman farmers. The Federalists condemned the brutal excesses of the French Revolution and its hungry guillotine. The Republicans applauded them. Federalists were most numerous in the commercial centers of the Northeast. Republicans were more noticeable in rural areas of the south and west. The Republicans sought as much individual freedom as possible and limited government. Federalists were more willing to use the tools of government for what they saw as the common good.

It is said some citizens are conservative by nature, in the sense they cling tightly to the almighty *Status Quo*. They seem born with a vigorous distaste for most forms of governmental action. Of a different temperament are the liberal-minded. They are disposed to think lightly of the risks and inconveniences that often attend social, political, and economic adjustments. Liberals are likely to give *every* change credit for being an improvement.

Just as today, these sentiments were prevalent in the nation's youth. They are attendants of the human psyche and form core compulsions for parties and politics in America. As for political parties, political scientist E. E. Schallsclmeider offered the following observation in 1942:

> Political parties created democracy and... modern democracy is unthinkable, save in terms of parties. The parties are not merely appendages of modern government; they are in the center of it and play a determinative role in it.

It is the writer's view—take issue if you will—that America's two-party system contributes greatly to stability of this remarkably stable Republic. Since 1790 the country has shown extraordinary stability. It swings neither far right nor left, as evidenced by the wrecks and wreckage of the Goldwater and McGovern campaigns for president. No banana republic here. Ideas and proposals that catch the eyes of voters are soon gobbled up, adopted, and incorporated into the platforms and programs of either or both major parties. The end result is immoderate third parties and third-party candidates are short-lived.

The Federalist versus Republican rivalry endured through the presidential election of 1816. That year Republican James Monroe, age 61, captured the White House, and the Federalist party ceased to exist. By and by the Republican party split into two divisions, designated "nationalist" and "democratic." Supporters of Andrew Jackson, elected president in 1828, dropped the Republican label and called themselves simply the Democratic Party.

Jackson was a strong president with a forceful agenda. In time his party became associated with the common man, free of the Jeffersonian fear of government power. President Jackson insisted upon expansion of the suffrage, rotation in office, the spoils system, and reliance upon confidence of the people.

The Jackson administration was accompanied by another important spectacle— the age of mass politics. Democrats endorsed use of the national nominating convention. In prior elections presidential candidates were chosen by congressional caucus. The convention system brought a growing number of everyday citizens into the political process.

With demise of the Federalist party, many of the country's conservatives became Whigs. They held together on opposition to "executive tyranny" and a varied program that included protective tariffs and a national bank. Their candidates for president won elections in 1840 and again in 1848. Party membership included a one-term congressman from Illinois named Abraham Lincoln.

The Age of Whiggery was brief. The party was unable to withstand growth of sectional differences and passed off the stage. In its place came forth the Republicans. They first offered a presidential candidate in 1856 and lost. They nominated Lawyer Lincoln in 1860, won the White House, and have remained Republicans ever since, symbolized by—of all things—a long-snouted wild elephant.

A Short Epilogue

George Washington. The first president resisted extensive urging to seek a third term in office. He retired and returned, after an absence of eight years, to his beloved estate on the Potomac River. Mount Vernon enveloped five separate farms tended by 200 slaves and overseers. It was the largest and most advanced farming operation in America. Its master, along with Roswell Garst and the Wallaces of Iowa, was one of the greatest farmers, in a nation that has excelled at agriculture as no other on earth.

On July 7, 1799, five months before his death, Washington redrew his last will and testament. It ran to twenty-eight pages. Among other things, it provided for the freedom of all Mount Vernon slaves upon the death of his loyal wife, Martha, {who survived him by five years}. He instructed his executors to meet this obligation "...without evasion, neglect or delay..." He was then 67 and had served at the forefront of the country's public life for two full decades.

Visitors by the droves traveled uninvited to Mount Vernon, where the aging master invariably hosted a large meal at 2 o'clock in the afternoon. All guests were seated. Jefferson once said of the man that he was incapable of physical fear. He and others noted that no one could sit astride a horse with the dignity of George Washington, widely regarded as one of the finest horsemen in America.

It was after a cold, wet ride that he returned to the mansion feeling unwell. In the early hours of December 14, 1799, he awoke feeling much worse and convinced he was fatally stricken. Until the end he cooperated with hurriedly summoned doctors, all the while giving final instructions to house servants and overseers. Nearing the end he was heard to whisper, "I die hard, but I am ready to go." When he passed into the void without a single complaint, a bed-side witness turned and testified, "Verily, a great man bath fallen this day in Israel."

John Adams. A holder of unquestionable revolutionary credentials, he became second president in 1796. A brilliant mind, a good man, and one of the best lawyers in early America, he proved a mediocre president. He had no executive experience and lacked the politician's necessary touch to serve in the executive office. He lost a bid for re-election to his own vice president, Thomas Jefferson, in the bitter partisan campaign of 1800.

Though an ineffective president, history has been generous to Adams. It has granted him high stature as one of America's greatest statesmen. He earned it fair and square for abiding allegiance to the public interest {as he saw it}, outstanding diplomatic service, unrelenting efforts toward independence, and a masterful contribution to the war effort through service on congressional committees ministering to the continental army. He died at his farm in Massachusetts on July 4, 1826, age 91.

[Note: The Twelfth Amendment, as adopted September 25, 1804, was drawn to prevent a reoccurrence of a presidential contest pitting a president of one party against his vice president of another. It has fulfilled that intent.]

Thomas Jefferson, third president. He receives high marks for his two-term administration. Through strong leadership, he expanded the national domain with the Louisiana Purchase, perhaps his greatest accomplishment. He conceived the three-year Lewis and Clark Expedition {one of the most successful in history}, and he oversaw a period of population growth, industrial expansion, and improvements in education. His mind and pen were probably the finest among the finest. Abraham Lincoln adjudged him America's greatest politician.

The Jeffersonian mystique, however, contained concealed features. They were marked with hypocrisy that has grown glaringly conspicuous with the passage of time. Public statements on his party's political aims, together with his writings and utterances on slavery, were in pointed contradiction to his private behavior at Monticello and ambitions to become president. He sat out the Revolutionary War on his Virginia plantation where he declined one or more requests for assistance from the heavily burdened Commander of the Continental Army. While vice president in the Adams administration, he worked behind the scenes to lay the groundwork for a presidential campaign against his sitting president.

Surrounded at Monticello by servants and a stream of important guests and visitors, he conducted a lavish, sedentary life style of correspondence, contemplation, rich food, and imported wines. He died dead broke July 4, 1826, age 82. His debts totaled $100,000, more at the time than the combined value of his magnificent house, his plantation and all its slaves, of which there were many, including Jefferson's own offspring whom he ignored. For you see, readers, in the depths and darkness of the slave world status of the child was determined by its mother.

James Madison. A revolutionary of the first rank, indispensable at the Constitutional Convention, by any measurement a great politician and constitutional lawyer. He, too, proved an undistinguished president during a two-term administration from 1809 to 1817. Thereafter, he lived quietly in retirement at Montpelier, his 5,000 acre Virginia plantation. He died there in 1836, age 85.

Alexander Hamilton. A great lawyer, writer, statesman, and patriot, his services to the republic were enormous, indeed. At the end of Washington's first term, he left public office and resumed law practice in New York, where his statue stands today on Wall Street. Despite demands of a busy practice, Hamilton maintained a vigorous correspondence concerning candidates, campaigns, and elections at the federal level. At the peak of his powers, he died a foolish death at age 49 in a duel with his personal, professional, and political rival—Vice President Aaron Burr. The date was July 11, 1804. He left behind a wife and seven children. Throughout the land his death was viewed as an immense perdition of the nation. As only Aline Jones Thomas of Pierce County, Georgia could sum it up, "What a loss! What a waste!"

An American President's Improbable Story

From the **Athens Banner Herald, February 12, 2013**

The legendary story had its beginnings on Feb. 12, 1809, in a rude cabin in Hardin County, Kentucky. A male child was born to an impoverished couple struggling for survival on the western edge of the wild American frontier. They wrapped him in a buffalo robe and named him Abraham, after his grandfather, whom Indians stalked and murdered in the Kentucky Territory twenty-five years earlier.

A father of meager means and a mother who died when he was nine left little that shaped his psyche. As a boy, however, a wise and caring stepmother, herself illiterate, encouraged his love for books and reading.

He was admitted to the bar in 1836 as a self-taught lawyer. Among other things, he had been a farmhand, oarsman on a Mississippi River flatboat, postmaster, store clerk, surveyor, and a member of the Illinois General Assembly.

He then surfaced on the Illinois prairie at Springfield, his possessions stuffed in two saddlebags. With his future wife's cousin, John T. Stuart, he formed a law partnership and his life took a new turn. Inordinately tall at 6 feet, 4 inches, and a compulsive raconteur, he was not much of a lawyer to begin with. Undeterred, he studied and worked at it. By 1850, he and his then-partner, William H. Herndon, claimed one of the best practices in the state, including representation of the Illinois Central Railroad.

From his first bid for elective office at age 23—which he lost in a field of thirteen candidates—and throughout life, politics remained an enduring passion. He pored over newspapers, pondered issues of the day, canvassed for candidates far and wide, offered repeatedly for the state legislature and once for Congress. Herndon called him "the most ambitious politician I ever saw."

In law and politics, he perceived instinctively the latent powers of public speech. Contrary to popular belief, he was never widely read, but he read the right stuff— rules of grammar and rhetoric, Webster's speeches, Euclid's geometry, the Bible, Byron's poetry, Shakespeare's plays and sonnets. He became a formidable stump speaker, courtroom advocate, and a stylist of the first rank.

A brooding, fatalistic, political genius, beset by recurring bouts of depression, politics failed to fully satisfy him. He served four terms as an undistinguished Illinois legislator and one-term Whig congressman, 1848-1850. He retired from public life in 1850 and resumed law practice with uncommon vigor.

Passage of the Kansas-Nebraska Act in May 1854, combined with the gathering national crisis, aroused him emotionally, politically, and intellectually. In 1858, he challenged the unsinkable Stephen A. Douglas in a U.S. Senate race.

During the Lincoln-Douglas debates he articulated better than any politician the moral force against slavery. Adopting Webster's words he declared, "A house divided... cannot stand."

He lost the election, but his speeches resonated. Those speeches, and the landmark Cooper Union address in New York City in 1860, stirred the newly-formed Republican Party. The national convention in Chicago that summer nominated him for president. With civil war sentiment spreading uncontrollably, the country elected a prairie lawyer as its Sixteenth President. He did not hunt, owned no firearms, abhorred the sight of blood—rumor had it he resisted chopping off the head of the Sunday chicken—and readily confessed to having no knowledge of military science.

Fort Sumter soon erupted. The southern states seceded and the war came. In the towering chaos, the president in his stovepipe hat became the central figure. Amidst rank radicalism, a war of unprecedented violence, civic crisis, and abuse and excoriation heaped upon him, he governed the union. All the while he directed the war effort, becoming a master strategist.

With the stillness at Appomattox, his works were made clear. He had secured the peace, preserved the Union, freed the slaves, won re-election, and passed the 13th Amendment, with words and speeches that burned into the English language and the American consciousness. General Henry W. Halleck, among witnesses at his bedside on the night of the assassination said, "No other living soul could have done it."

In the beginning a nobody from nowhere; in the end, a self-educated lawyer, legislator, politician, president and wartime leader, one whose service to the republic reached epic dimensions, that was and is Abraham Lincoln.

Odds Were Against the American Revolution

From the Athens Banner-Herald, July 6, 2013

John Adams, Boston lawyer, revolutionary leader, influential diplomat, and the Second President, described the events of 237 years ago this month as "the most memorable epoch in the history of America." Few, if any, disagree.

Adams was pointing, to a single five-month period from May to October 1776. Author Joseph Ellis calls it the "revolutionary summer in America." It was a time in which the Second Continental Congress severed its ties with Britain, then on July 4, published the Declaration of Independence. That date became Independence Day, a paid federal holiday since 1938.

An event of equal import occurred six years after end of the Revolutionary War. In May 1787, delegates to the Constitutional Convention began drafting and debating a constitution to replace the ineffective Articles of Confederation. A century later, William Gladstone praised their written instrument as "the greatest work ever struck off at a given time by the brain and purpose of man."

Both landmark chapters of American history are the more memorable—in retrospect implausible—in view of conditions from which they arose. That each gave rise to individual revolutionaries and political geniuses was as unexpected and remarkable as any events in history.

Colonial America was small and thinly populated. Historians estimate the population in 1776 at 2.5 million, less than the population of San Diego County today. A quarter of the inhabitants were African slaves. The population of New York was 33,131; Philadelphia had 28,522 residents, and Boston a mere 18,320. Otherwise the inhabitants, mainly small farmers, were widely scattered along the eastern seaboard from Georgia to Vermont.

Misery and poverty abounded. Life expectancy lasted less than 50 years. The few brave travelers, George Washington among them, who jostled their way cross-country were appalled at the deplorable state of roads, bridges, housing, roadside taverns and inns.

Most colonists were poorly educated, if at all. Outside Boston, New York, and Philadelphia, books were scarce, as were schools. Only seven colleges offered degrees. Their graduates numbered 4,400—about two for every thousand white persons.

Communications, the medium of politics, were as dilatory as those of Roman times—by foot, horseback, stage-coach, and sailing vessel.

As subjects of King George III, the colonists had no flag, no anthem, no capitol city, and no president. Beginning about 1763, however, grassroots agitation for separation from the mother country began reverberating. "Liberty" became the shock word of the times. By 1775, the colonists were engaged in a bloody insurrection aimed at overthrowing British rule and replacing it with a new order.

A favorable outcome was never guaranteed, and it was dangerous in the extreme. One can lose one's head in a revolution. "If you smite at the King," said Machiavelli, "you better kill him."

Revolutions demand of their leaders profound convictions, unimpeachable integrity, and unwavering courage. Political skills, a capacity to sprout and spread propaganda, a willingness to employ weapons and an ability to cope with profound personal risks are insurrectionist and revolutionary.

Very few possess such skills and convictions; rustic, struggling, tiny colonial America produced a collection of them. They included superb orators, writers, thinkers, and men of action who were educated and widely read. Many were steeped in the writings of the period's prominent political philosophers, statecraft, if you will, namely John Locke of England and Montesquieu of France.

Atop the revolutionary pyramid were Alexander Hamilton, Thomas Jefferson, John Adams, Sam Adams,

Patrick Henry, James Madison, John Jay, and George Mason. Thomas Paine with his pamphlet, "Common Sense," proved the revolutionary propagandist par excellence. Also espousing total independence was the one indispensable man, George Washington, together with perhaps the wisest of the lot, Benjamin Franklin.

Unlike many of history's armed insurrections, the American Revolution did not "eat its own children." On the contrary, with few exceptions, they survived and joined a set of political geniuses too numerous to name as delegates to the Constitutional Convention, assembled at Independence Hall in Philadelphia. Washington, Adams, Jefferson, and Madison later became presidents.

Once more the best and brightest appeared on the scene, though for many the arduous trip to Philadelphia was weeks in duration. Two centuries later, we are still the beneficiaries of the wise works of these extraordinarily gifted men.

Taxes, Taxation, and the Super-Rich

From the Macon Telegraph, July 31, 2011

Greater parts of the citizenry acknowledge their good fortune. They are lucky to live in America. Most love their country. And, like me, I believe many are mystified, distraught and outraged at the array of uncalled for misfortunes that have set upon us. They threaten living standards, social and economic advancement, and the innate sense of fairness ingrained in the American character.

Hard to believe, isn't it? A little more than two decades ago, the Soviet Union collapsed. America won the Cold War and became the world's sole super power. Her military and economic strengths stood at heights unknown since Roman times, in the era of Octavian.

Boom Times

We then set off on a great ride for the mega-rich and excessively compensated executives. Beginning in the 1980s and continuing pretty much unencumbered until 2008—irrespective of two wars on the other side of the globe — the economy grew, the job market expanded. Interest rates were low. Gas was cheap, relatively speaking, and the value of homes appreciated year after year. The stock market created massive amounts of new wealth, as the word "billionaire" came into common usage, The Dow Jones industrial average climbed from 803 in the summer of 1982 to 14,165 in the fall of 2007.

Bum Times

Look at America today. Not only is her dress tattered and her beautiful face dirty, but she is swamped in debt. Neither Republicans nor Democrats appear capable of handling her finances. A claque of misguided, unreasonable, howling partisans in the U.S. House have gridlocked and stalled the government.

Trust in Congress has fallen below that of Wall Street. According to Senate Minority Leader Mitch McConnell, (R-Ky.), for the first time since Gallup began polling in 1935, a majority of Americans believe the best times are behind us.

Three short years ago, the highest-ranking government officials reported the nation was on the brink of financial collapse.

With the bursting of the housing bubble, Americans became reacquainted with the harsh meaning of the word "foreclosure." Gary Schilling, an economic consultant with A. Gary Shilling & Co., is credited with predicting the 2008 housing crash. He now predicts a 20 percent decline in home values in 2011.

Middle Class Woes

Times are hard for both the middle class and those in poverty. Yes, poverty, with its damning effects on lives, old and young. The level has risen to 14.3 percent. In Georgia, 534,000 children are living in poverty. In Washington, D.C., 18.8 percent of its children are living in extreme poverty. Need we remind ourselves; this is not Pakistan, Bangladesh, or Mozambique.

As for the largest segment of Americans, those of the middle class, the economy is not working well and has not for a generation. American households are putting in more job time than ever. Among working-age married couples with children, the extra hours total 10 additional full-time weeks at work, when compared to 1979.

Though the economy grew significantly between 1979 and 2006, the middle class, laboring as never before, realized a grand income gain of just 0.7 percent a year. Society's top tier netted a 10 percent gain.

CEO Enrichment

While middle-class workers strain at making ends meet, the chief executive officers of the nation's top companies continue reaping a bonanza. In 1960, CEO pay was 42 times higher than their workers. By 2007, it rose to 411 times greater than wages, reports the University of California at Santa Cruz.

But it doesn't end there. In 2010, the median pay of America's CEOs jumped 27 percent, from $7.1 million in 2009 to $9 million, based on the Standard and Poor's 500 Index. The evidence is in the record. For a generation, the bottom rung of earners went nowhere. The struggling middle class eked our modest gains. The mega-rich ran off with all the money.

For those who care for their country, do yourselves a favor and read Jacob Hacker's and Paul Pierson's new book, *Winner Take All Politics*. They lay it out for all to see, who are willing to see.

A few radicals aside, Americans do not detest the rich. On the contrary, they admire them and revere their success. Aspirations for wealth, the dream and desire "to get rich" are as prevalent as pine trees in Georgia. Money is how we keep score in America. No elected leader, clique, faction, or party seeks to restrict one iota those timeless ambitions. Furthermore, the mere rich are outside the discussion.

Why Tax the Mega-Rich?

But here is what is happening. Look at the top 1 percent of the country's richest, more particularly the upper levels of the 1 percent. I refer to those whose wealth exceeds all need, all reason, all sanity. These are the billionaires and the lesser lights whose treasures only measure in the hundreds of millions. Their share of national income has grown from 9 percent in 1974 to 23.5 percent.

In terms of assets rather than income, the top 1 percent controls an estimated 40 percent of the wealth. Think what that means in a nation of 310 million. Hard to believe, but true; the richest 400 Americans own more wealth than the bottom 150 million Americans.

They grow ever richer. In the period 2002-2007, the top 0.1 percent was in the upper tier of the 1 percent of all earners.

The congressional Republicans insist it is fair. Speaker John Boehner and his claque of colleagues adamantly refuse all marginal, fair and prudent adjustments to the American tax system. To protect billionaires, they are willing to close down the U.S. government and risk another global crisis.

Do the Mega-Rich Create Jobs?

They say it's the super rich who stimulate growth and create jobs. If so, why haven't they? Almost a full decade ago, while waging two wars costing billions, and while asking nothing to pay for costs in the trillions, President George W. Bush and the Republicans passed a massive reduction in marginal tax rates, a reduction that has benefited the wealthy greatly in excess of other taxpayers, while contributing immeasurably to the national debt.

We were told reduced tax revenue would accelerate business growth and produce more jobs. By now, for every thinking citizens, the haggard truth is out. The wealth did not "trickle down," according to Republican supply-side economics.

The country has endured years of anemic job growth, stagnant wages, declining incomes, and a monumental escalation of distorted income inequality. The super rich have prospered. Those who live from paycheck to paycheck have not.

The times and the circumstances demand it. We must have a sensible tax system, a system that is fair, equitable, and just, one that reflects the growing stratification in American incomes.

Is it too much to ask of those who have benefitted so greatly to return a marginal tax amount to the nation?

The Greatest Fix of All

F rom the Dublin Courier-Herald, July 13, 2011

Among city dwellers in particular, but widespread in the popular mind, is the misbelief that the greatest fix of all is the *drug fix* (DF). That is; the use and ingestion of heroine, crack cocaine, methamphetamine, morphine, hashish, opium, opiod, the lowly joint. The misbelief has an evidentiary basis.

Narcotics have deluged the culture. Millions crave their euphoric rush and shell out $113 billion annually (at last count) to buy the stuff. Unrestricted to addled brains, the DF perpetuates social rot, enriches dregs-of-the-earth dealers, incites a War on Drugs, and continues cramming penitentiaries with perpetrators. One is wont to conclude the DF has to be the most potent fix of all. As we shall see, however, the DF lags the *greatest fix of all* (GFOA)—by a mile. Comparing the two is like comparing a field mouse to a Bangkok elephant.

Unknown for the most part, the GFOA is the *nitrogen fix* (NF). Yes, nitrogen (N_2), Number 7 on the Periodic Table. In 1909 in the chemistry laboratory at a technical institute at Karlsruhe, Germany, during an era when Germany was at the forefront of chemical science, an extraordinarily talented chemist developed a new technology for taping into the atmosphere and extracting nitrogen, in the form of liquid ammonia. Industry could then convert, or "fix" the ammonia into compounds suitable for plant food, i.e. nitrogen-based additives spread on growing crops. Fritz Haber's earth-shattering breakthrough was soon producing prodigious benefits, and continued to across the twentieth-century.

Discovery of the GFOA proved one of man's supreme scientific and technological achievements. Yet, it remains one of the least appreciated in human history. All the more astonishing when as historian of science Stephen R. Brown says: "Two fifths of the world's current population would not be here but for the [GFOA]... global dependence on it will only increase as world population grows to between 9 and 10 billion by mid-century."

The most significant scientific feat of the twentieth century? "Yes," answer many of the well-informed. They say it outranks nuclear energy, airplanes, television, computers, and space flight. Among those of this view is one Vaclav Smil. In 2010 *Foreign Policy* magazine placed him on its roster of top global thinkers. A distinguished professor of the history of agriculture and environmental science, and a Fellow of the Royal Society of Canada, he writes in his influential book, *Enriching the Earth*, "...that none of these inventions has been as fundamentally important as the... [GFOA]. Lives of the world's 6 billion people might actually be better without Microsoft Windows and 600 TV channels, and neither nuclear reactors nor space shuttles are critical determinants of human well being."

Smil places his finger directly on point: People can do without most comforts and conveniences intrinsic to this frantic age; nourishment of their mortal bodies they cannot.

As for nitrogen, what is it anyhow? For starters, it floats in the air we breathe. U.S industry produces more of it than any other chemical. An essential nutrient of food-producing vegetation, its availability determines the productivity of entire food systems. Its other properties, too, are worth noting:

- Nitrogen is found in every cell of all living things and is present at every level of biological function;
- Fixed nitrogen is required to biosynthesize the basic building blocks of life, e.g., nucleotides for DNA and RNA and amino acids for proteins;
- It comprises eighty percent of Earth's atmosphere;
- A free agent, it circulates through the air, soils, plants, and animals, as an inert, stable, odorless, colorless gas;

- On every square mile of Earth's surface, rest 22,000 tons of it, rendering the total amount nearly 4 billion tons;
- Bacteria in soils produce nitrates that are "taken up" by growing plants. Plant vitality is limited by the levels of nitrogen bacteria can provide;
- Supplementing soil nitrates with man-made nitrogen additives enhances yields in food-producing field crops.

(Aside from bacterial action in soils and some aquatic bacteria, lightning strikes are one of earth's few phenomena that produce fixed nitrogen.)

At turn of the twentieth century, mastery of nitrogen fixation had become an enigma of the age, the Holy Grail of scientific research. Warnings were being sounded that population growth would soon outpace food production; that a desperate need existed for more reliable supplies of nitrates. A gigantic upsurge in demand for nitrates (compounds of sodium nitrate or potassium nitrates) in civil engineering and warfare, combined with the predictions of famine, moved nitrogen research to the forefront of scientific inquiry. (The explosives and munitions industries were huge consumers of nitrates, hence major participants in the nitrogen drama. Though touched upon in this piece, their full effects are best described elsewhere.)

Adding to the demand for nitrates were warnings of shortages. Fortunately, Haber's discovery was soon forthcoming. Before close of the century's first decade, in an epic saga of human ingenuity, chemistry, and experimentation, he found a way to split off the strong nitrogen hydrogen molecules found in ammonia (NH_3). The GFOA thus became a reality. (The word, "fix," is alchemical in origin and first recorded in English in 1393. In chemistry it denotes the conversion of something volatile and mobile to a solid form. Contemporary chemists rarely use the word.)

Named the "Haber-Process" after its inventor, Germany industrialized it with astonishing speed and engineering proficiency. The first manufacturing plant was soon producing nitrogen- based products for the fertilizer industry. (The word "fertilizer" means any natural or manufactured material added to soils to increase plant growth.) When applied to growing plants, the effects of nitrogen-based fertilizer are clearly visible. Growth is promptly invigorated. Leaves enlarge and turn a darker green. Aging of the plant is slowed. Though invisible in the cereal grains, nitrogen affects the size and content of proteins.

Haber-Process let loose a tide of synthetic plant food. The tide released farmers from their aged dependency on elusive, often inadequate, malodorous supplies of nitrates. They consisted mainly of organic substances—human waste, liquid and solid, barnyard manures and urinary additives—all essential in the everlasting cycle of seedtime and harvest.

The GFOA elevated food production to undreamed of heights. It leveled an assault on the persistent evils of famine and want, all the while improving diet, bodily comforts, and extending life spans. And brought forth from the earth by an ever-shrinking farmer population, in the U.S. anyway. In the second decade of the twenty-first century, his average age is 57.5 years. He feeds 338 souls. Before the GFOA he fed two.

Turning from invention to the inventor, who was Fritz Haber, the central figure of this drama? He was professor of physical chemistry and electrochemistry and director of the Technical Institute at the University of Karlsruhe, at Karlsruhe, Germany (an academic and research institution). Brilliant, highly motivated, still in his 30s, Haber was approaching the apex of an exemplary career. Beginning in 1907, and working from a professional position virtually non-existent in either science or academia outside Germany, Haber turned his formidable intellect full bore on the nitrogen fixation problem. Success came less than two years later.

Back to Fritz Haber the man and the chemist. He was a prominent figure in German chemistry and technical education, The son of a prosperous Prussian Jewish merchant, he was polylingual, broadly educated in the arts and classics, versatile in talents, remarkably knowledgeable of politics, economics, and industry. Though clearly qualified for success in other fields, he lived for science. In addition he was highly ambitious, competitive, and an inexhaustible worker, as evidenced by publication of more than 50 scientific papers between 1900 and 1905. On his students—who came from all over the world—he left lasting impressions as a man of science and as an empathetic mentor.

And so in 1907 Haber and his able collaborator, Alois Mittasch, launched their nitrogen-fixation experiments. Others chemists had tried and failed but nevertheless made progress. And, once made, advances in science are rarely lost. For instance, researchers knew that electric charges can produce ammonia. Chemists Ramsey and Young discovered that decomposition of ammonia in a hot tub is temperature dependent. Haber and Mittasch scrutinized these findings.

Haber and Mittasch diligently pursued their laboratory experiments. They tested an astonishing 2,500 different catalysts, while adjusting and readjusting temperatures and pressures. They pumped hydrogen and nitrogen through pressurized canisters. By July 1909 they had assembled a table-top apparatus capable of producing synthetic ammonia. Its circulating system, operating continuously at raised temperatures, produced a steady stream of it at the rate of 80 grams per hour.

Sodium nitrate, ammonium sulfate, anhydrous ammonia, ammonium nitrate, urea—farmers applied them to field crops in staggering amounts. World-wide production of synthetic ammonia rose to 100 million tons annually. It then rose again. By 2001 it reached 130 million tons. That amounts to 110 million tons of fixed nitrogen, of which agriculture consumes four- fifths. Indeed, one of the world's largest industries produces a principal ingredient in man's everlasting quest for food sufficiency.

The evidence is conclusive. Haber's invention affected the foundations of human existence. By elevating agricultural productivity to the levels achieved, the German chemist precipitated the deepest transformation of the last century. Perhaps of any other. Where would we be without the GFOA?

Afterword

As for Frritz Haber, his attention was directed toward pursuits aside from the peaceful. It was he, benefactor of humanity, scientist of the Kaiser, German patriot through and through, who conceived, developed, and *directed* one of the premier horrors of World War I—gas warfare. It earned him condemnations that still linger. For his wartime initiatives the intense strong-willed chemist rejected all moral responsibility. He asserted there was no distinction between dying of gas and from a bullet.

After Karlsruhe Haber became director of the prestigious Kaiser Wilhelm Institute in Berlin where he was totally devoted to scientific research. On April 7, 1933, the Nazis overlooked his Jewish descent but demanded dismissal of his staff of Jewish scientists. In a display of iron-clad integrity, he refused and resigned. His letter of resignation reads in part "...in a scientific post in choosing fellow workers, I take into account only professional qualifications and the character of the applicant..." Haber went into exile and died the following year, en route from England to convalescence in Switzerland following a serious illness. He was 66.

Integrity: Essential Ingredient of Civic Trust

In an Opinion piece, Editor Bert Roughton pointed to diminished public trust in institutions of government, business, non-profits, the media, as well as their leaders. Drawing from recent surveys by the Edelman Trust Barometer, he wrote, "Bad things happen when leaders lack public trust," He cited failure of Georgia's transportation referendum as a case in point.

The Edelman data, by the way, shows that less than one-fifth of the general public believes business leaders will tell the truth when confronted with a difficult problem. Only ten percent believe politicians are truthful when under stress.

Civic concern is justified. Public trust does matter. It undergirds confidence in public policy, the quality of leadership, the value of goods and services, the credibility of communications around the globe. .The Wall Street Journal reported that as European Union leaders head for a summit meeting "...they face a crisis harder to fix than their debt problem...a loss of trust in the European Union itself."

Among other things Mr. Roughton urged an 'agenda of greater integrity.'

Agreed; performance with integrity forms the foundation of trust and reputation. Now more than ever it has no downside and cannot be over emphasized. For ours is a frantic hyper-connected age of non-stop media and internet transparency. Everything lodges in cyberspace, and somebody somewhere is always watching.

If public and private leaders are to embrace enhanced integrity, they do well to probe and grasp the essence of it—in the abstract and in practice. Not surprisingly, it is easier to identify than define.

The word itself comes at us from every point on the compass. And, yet, as former US Senator Bill Bradley of New Jersey observes, "Few pause to define it, or to describe its contributions to everyday life." In 2005, MerriamWebster reported that on its renowned dictionary website it was the one word most sought for definition. Even fewer search for the tenets governing it until confronted with being compromised.

In substance the virtue radiates adhesion. It mandates adherence to principles that withstand moral scrutiny, that are beneficial to the parties involved. Pared to the core, integrity is an uncompromising loyalty to the right ideas—even when it is inconvenient, difficult, or unprofitable. Integrity encompasses the right choice, at the right time, for the right reason, albeit no law, rule or regulation, requires it.

Said Albert Camus, "If you have integrity you don't even need the rules."

Here is how it looks up close. Integrity is an imperative for institutional leaders who place a premium on trustworthiness and reputation; keep their word in matters great and small; ascribe a heavy weight to accountability; deliver as promised, when promised, in the manner promised; are willing to stand up and be counted when it counts; refuse to play fast and loose with the rules; exert scrupulous honesty; tell the truth regardless of the consequences, knowing that even when it hurts it will help; they accept that *how* they perform is as critical as *what* they perform.

These were ingredients Ray Croc employed as founder of McDonald's. In 1954, he owned the rights to market a commercial milkshake machine. From his office in Chicago he traveled much of the country observing the operations of fast food and short order restaurants. Later, he admitted to having eaten a great deal of "fast food." As the years passed, Croc formulated a conviction that three essentials of the dining experience were Quality, Service, and Cleanliness. He labeled his credo the QSC

As chief executive of McDonald's, QSC became Ray Croc's guiding standard. No one could cite an instance of his veering from it, compromising it, or failing to enforce it. (He was often seen cleaning the bathrooms when visiting a store.) McDonald's employees trusted their chief explicitly because he lived what he believed, and stood by what he said, and preached it wherever he went. The yellow arches sprouting all over the nation were proof of the benefits.

Croc demonstrated integrity's timeless and timely message. Integrity enforces purpose. It generates commitment. It strengthens standards at all levels, encourages adherence to values, and defeats the ill-advised compromise. Trust is a priceless by-product. May responsible leaders everywhere hold ever tighter to it.

Rules of Compromise–Reconsidered

In Washington deadlocked government exhibits political conflict in the extreme. On conflict in general, however, the politicians hold no monopoly. Both useful and fraught with risks, conflicts develop at every turn, a by-product of modem life's divisions, distresses and strife.

Proposals for change, whatever the setting, are rarely accepted by acclamation. Instead, the parties stake out positions for and against and bargaining begins. It differs from other forms of bargaining, for the objective becomes getting to "yes," of reaching an acceptable resolution. That either side must be happy with the outcome is immaterial.

The process is known as "compromise," a shock word of the twenty-first century. The entire subject is rich and complicated. Directly applicable, however, are three universal principles, or tenets. Where understood and utilized they heighten prospects of a workable compromise. Lord Morley identified them in 1877 in his landmark work, *Compromise*.

The participants at the bargaining table bring to the fray fixed mindsets, a collection of preconceived opinions and beliefs. They fall into three distinct departments: the formation of opinion and belief; the expression and publication of them; the impulse to see them put into practice.

Tenet one holds that in forming a belief there are no differences to split. The basis for a given belief may emanate from many sources. After all we live in the information age. But, in making up one's mind in the first place the truth of the matter is non-negotiable. He who is honest with himself knows the truth cannot lie; between it and falsehood there can be no synthesis. In deciding what to believe, nothing is as probative as the unassailable fact, the indisputable evidence. The sun does not rise in the east one day and in the west the next.

When it comes to expressing beliefs, compromise is less absolute. So says tenet two.

Why express one's beliefs at all? Because words matter. When grounded in truth and prudently declared they penetrate, even in the minds of opponents. The time is always right to publish the truth. On the other hand, the wise choice of time and place is also authorized.

Beliefs and opinions—openly and freely spoken—affect permanent change. Their publication lays the platform for practical application of initiatives that are unfamiliar, weighty, yet promising. Does any reasonable person believe Congress would have passed The Affordable Care Act had proponents of national health insurance not openly espoused it for decades?

It is often said that he who begins life by stifling his convictions is well along the road for ending it with no convictions to stifle.

It is one thing to form a belief and another to express it. A different dilemma arises when striving to implement it. Here tenet three allows for still greater flexibility.

Herbert Spencer said, "There is an indispensable compromise between old ideas and old institutions as opposed to new ideas as perceived by their advocates."

New ideas are forever launched against the almighty, seemingly impregnable, status quo, which lest we forget, was implanted by reformers, agitators, liberals, and, yes, radicals of ages past. In the realization of the strongest held beliefs, there is no prohibition against accepting a partial adoption of it—so long as the partial adoption is in the direction of total adoption. The tactic to quash lies in accepting part of it for all of it, thereby eliminating further need for implementation.

Senator Wayne Morse of Oregon was a strong advocate of civil rights legislation throughout his long career in public life. Yet, he was the only senator outside the Deep South who voted against the 1957 Civil Rights Act, a bill that contained expanded liberties for minorities in housing and education. He did so because in his view, "This bill does not go far enough."

The art of compromise, so essential in modern life, is

no easy task. Morley's three tenets will prove beneficial, provided, adversaries put aside small calculations, petty utilities, search for the highest truths, and cling to them above all else. Each tenet necessitates the exercise of judgment, joined to an overpowering consideration of the greater good. And "Judgment," said Abraham Lincoln, "is of greater value than brilliance."

Genocide, Nuremberg,
and the Shame of the West

From The Dublin Courier-Herald, August 18, 2010

Time Magazine recently published an account of injustice that should have, but did not, rouse world leaders throughout the West.

In Phnom Penh, one Kaing Geuk Eav, known as "Duch" was found guilty of crimes against humanity. A jailer and torture chief, one who oversaw the deaths of at least 14,000 during the Khmer Rouge's murderous reign, Duch received a nineteen-year sentence. Families of victims wept in outrage. Civilized people everywhere should weep with them.

To date he is the only member of the "killing fields" regime to face justice. More than three decades after

Khmer Rouge slaughtered 1.7 million of its citizens, thirty years after the war crimes trials at Nuremberg, a single war criminal is prosecuted and given a limited sentence for genocide. His murderous satanic leader, Pol Pot, was never prosecuted and died of natural causes in 1998.

Crimes of passion are as old as history, not so genocide. It is the scourge of the twentieth century, and a word that did not exist until 1944. It means the deliberate, violent destruction, in whole or in part, of an ethnic, religious, national, or racial group. It involves the mass murder of innocent people, not for purposes of alteration but extermination.

Genocide is a war crime, a violation of international law. No nation, government, group, sect, or nationality, therefore, has the right to slaughter its citizens with impunity. That precedent was firmly fixed in a high point of western civilization—the war crimes trials at Nuremberg in 1945. It is a proven postulate of justice, an uncontradicted lesson of the last century. Inexplicably, the Nuremberg precedents are rarely mentioned, if at all, much less invoked and enforced.

Consider the evidence, Cambodia aside. In 1994, while the world watched from a distance, 800,000 Rwandans were slaughtered in a single 100-day period, many hacked to death with machetes and grubbing hoes. To date one culpable official was convicted and given a 25-year sentence. Former president Bill Clinton is on record as saying his failure to act was one of the regrets of his administration. How small the consolation.

In the Balkans in 1992-1995, more than 8,000 Muslim men and boys were murdered in a campaign of ethnic cleansing, carried out by Serb Forces in Srebrenica. The following May, with U.S. forces deployed in the Balkans, Richard Goldstone, chief prosecutor of the United Nations War Crimes Tribunal, made a special trip to the United States. He came to request of Secretary of State Warren Christopher that American troops be allowed to assist in the arrest of indicted war criminals. The secretary denied the request without a peep from the White House. Mr. Goldstone resigned his post and returned to South Africa.

In the Darfur region of the Sudan, yet another genocide is underway. This time at the hands of the Janjaweed, a government supported militia recruited from local Arab tribes. Thus far 400,000 have been exterminated. Five thousand die each month.

Where "at home and abroad" is the condemnation of these monstrosities? How can the highest leaders of the most advanced nations ignore the atrocities? Where is the will to enforce the rule of international law against genocide—wherever and whenever it occurs? If a given state cannot protect its citizens from wholesale butchery, the West has a duty to do it for them. For these crimes of butchery, boundary lines of states and nations are no defense.

And yes, the U.S. had a duty to lead. No other nation possesses its power and might, unknown since the time of Augustus. No other nation has greater or stronger traditions in the rule of law.

We have the right to expect and demand this from the president on down. Humanity has the right to expect it of America. Intervene, eradicate genocide, apprehend the wicked perpetrators, and hold them accountable. Enough is far more than enough.

Wickedness Demands Retribution

From The Dublin Courier-Herald, September19, 2001

The events of September 11 dictate a terrible mandate that American leadership appears to have fully grasped. This country must unleash its mighty powers against terrorism and bear the cost that entails-both in lives and material. The wickedness in New York and Washington demands retribution. Even more is required. **This time remember Nuremburg!**

The leadership cannot ignore the precedents set at Nuremburg half a century ago, at a frightful cost of blood and treasure in World War II. In a highpoint of Western Civilization, the trials of Nazi criminals established that assault on peaceful civilians is a war crime. So is genocide. Nuremburg holds that war criminals shall be held accountable. When captured, they shall be indicted, tried in a court of law, and, when found guilty, promptly executed.

In the post-Vietnam era, America lost its way and its will. It drove the Iraqi invaders from Kuwait and watched as they fired the priceless oil fields, leaving in their wake 900 burning wells. It was the greatest assault on the environment in recorded history.

The murderous Saddam Hussein and his court, however, acted with total impunity. Not one was indicted, much less arrested or tried. Nuremberg was shunned and forgotten.

A decade later, in Yugoslavia, America was content to bomb the Balkans to pieces. Amidst records of genocide, ethnic cleansing, and the bombardment of civilians in towns and cities, the leadership again abandoned the rule of law. It made no demands that the war criminals themselves be held accountable. United States soldiers deployed in the region were not even allowed to arrest those indicted by the United Nations' War Crimes Tribunal.

Our politicians somehow adopted an ill-founded notion where casualties were concerned. They acted as if America would not tolerate "body bags" regardless of the cause. A single loss of life was viewed as a national tragedy.

That is and was political nonsense. This is a great and mighty nation. It helped abate the mass slaughter of World War I. It helped save Western Civilization in World War II. It contained aggressive communism and won the Cold War. It stands preeminent, admired and unquestioned in a manner unknown since the time of Augustus. When called upon we will pay the necessary price to protect it.

The United States has the greatest traditions in the rule of law of any modern nation. Its capacity to enforce the rule of law is colossal. Our leaders, this time, must demand that the rule of law shall be enforced, without remorse or apology-to the last full measure.

By enforcing the rule of law, we check the ambitions of tyrants. We dissuade terrorists. We protect nature's necessary resources. We enhance human life and dignity. We have the right to expect this from our leadership. The civilized world and humanity have the right to expect it of America.

Enough criminality is enough.

High Stakes High Over England

From **The Dublin Courier-Herald, October 7, 2009**

This past September seventy-six years ago, a ground observer reported the skies over England were "...filled with screaming engines, explosions, white-hot tracers, burning airplanes, parachutes, and death." The Battle of Britain was raging toward its deadly apex. Life, as the British knew it, and Western Civilization were at extreme risk.

Today, the action is rapidly drifting into the mists of time and history, but for many in the West the events are still vivid. By the summer of 1940, a murderous German tyrant had forced most of western Europe under the jackboots of Hitlerian Satanism, France being his latest victim. England—alone, out-manned, and under armed—faced the next Nazi onslaught.

Generals of the Wehrmacht perceived that a successful cross-channel invasion turned on control of the air, as a deterrent to warships of the Royal Navy. The Luftwaffe, therefore, set out to demolish the Royal Air Force, and the battle was joined.

Confronting the enemy were three-thousand RAF pilots, in their Spitfires and Hurricane fighter planes. Rarely were more than nine-hundred available on any given day. The flyers were incredibly young, courageous, and highly motivated. Known as "the few" and commanded by the able Air Chief Marshal, Sir Hugh Dowding, their battle plan was settled: avoid pitched fights with the Luftwaffe's greater numbers; attack and destroy as many enemy bombers as possible; preserve the precious reserves of planes and pilots; and delay the invasion until October. By then the storm season in the channel would have set in. Wind and waves would render too hazardous the passage of an armed flotilla.

Though intensely questioned at times, Dowding's strategy triumphed and England held. While stretched to the limit of men and machines, the RAF shot down too many German bombers and fighter aircraft. The losses compelled Hitler to delay the invasion until it was too late. As the skies began to clear, Winston Churchill appeared on the cliffs of the English Channel and declared, "We are waiting on the invasion. So are the fishes."

Within the towering drama, however, is an often-unrecognized contingent—the RAF's volunteer pilots. They were volunteers, mind you, sensing the wind was up, that everything was riding on this one, and who migrated to

England and offered their services. They came from America, Canada, Poland, France, Czechoslovakia, South Africa, and Australia. Why did they do it?

One cannot testify on the mental state of others. No doubt, their motives were numerous, as the virtues of integrity and courage have many motivations. This we do know: there are those upright souls with characters of steel who can foresee the gravity of an occasion, the rightness of a cause, and irrespective of its dangers find participation exhilarating. Lying deep within the human psyche, it is a largely indescribable sentiment that emerges from knowing one is in "the fray when it is played for all the marbles."

A great college football coach came close to expressing it. When Bud Wilkinson was asked why he chose to come out of retirement late in life and coach the St. Louis Cardinals professional football team, he replied, "I wanted to experience again the intensity of the moment."

The antithesis of Wilkinson's mentality is found in a bronze plague on the wall of the Hotel de Crillon in Paris. The inscription dates from 1589, when King Henry IV of France won a bloody, important victory at the Battle of Argues, while his erstwhile friend, supporter and confidant stayed away. Henry sent him word, "Hang yourself, brave Crillon. We have fought at Argues, and you were not there."

It was Charles de Gaulle, speaking from a record of momentous works, who struck the vital vein. Said he, "There is no challenge of more grandeur than the meeting of a great crisis." The volunteer fighter pilots of 1940 met one of history's greatest crises, high in the skies over England. It cost one of three their lives, but they were there when it counted and helped present posterity an unprecedented 'grandeur.'

A Second Look at Second Chances

Texas Governor Rick Perry, on a tour probing possibilities for a repeat run at the White House, pressed the point that America is a *great place* for second chances. His predecessor and former president, George W. Bush, put it more decisively. He declared America *is the land* of second chances.

Both statements are equally valid. Second chances are an ingrained feature—tantamount to an ideal—in American life. Granting them in virtually all circumstances has wide approval. Conversely, they are denounced as too generously bestowed, as outrageously undeserved.

The Desolo Poll of February 2012 produced the following results.[1] Of those queried twenty-seven percent said they favored granting a second chance in all circumstances; thirty-two percent approved most of the time; thirty-six percent said half the time, depending

---

[1] Decolo Poll of February 2012 http://www.unexplained-mysteries.com/forum/index.php?showtopic=222236

on the circumstances; five percent said rarely; nobody said never.

The psychology turns on an ancient theme. Why do we give people second chances? Who deserves them? Who does not? Who is to say? The answers are not dictated.

The topic is multi-faceted, stuffed with nuance, and full of ambivalence. If it exists, controlling law remains hidden. No mind-set is certain, and distinctions must be drawn. An appraisal turns on the circumstances of any given case, in all respects save one: For those who grasp it for all they are worth, a second chance is one of life's supreme blessings.

They are not statistical and they come along all the time. One has a second chance to say "hello" to a stranger, to see the Yankees play, buy a stock, paint a house, read a book; perhaps less frequently a second chance at love. Said Mae West: "All discarded lovers should be given a second chance, but with somebody else."

In his autobiography, *Too Late to Say Goodbye*, Art Buchwald, describes his loss of virginity to the chambermaid who enticed him into a storage room at the Hotel Nassau in Long Beach, Long Island. He was fifteen and the year was 1941. Long afterwards, in a radio interview toward the end of his life, Buchwald admitted to being overly excited. "But," he added. "The dear lady graciously gave me a second chance."

Everyday second chances are not in question. Those that merit attention represent a contingency, a new con-

tingency laden with consequences. Not necessarily life-al-
tering or career-changing outcomes, though sometimes
that is precisely the case, but a conjuncture bearing
weight. One's quest, goal, ambition, campaign—some aim
and endeavor—for whatever reasons is denied, diverted,
squandered, miss-managed, damaged, stolen, or fails.
Events fall into place and a second chance opens. Once
more the aspirant pursues the original objective. Life is
arbitrary, as are second chances. They emanate from stark
fate, a roll of the dice, aid and intervention of third parties,
the electorate's forgiveness at the ballot box—indeed, from
every current, cross-current, and backwater of life's ever-
rolling stream. They emerge in a frantic age marked by
uncertainty, change, indissoluble calculations; an existence
of wasted and missed opportunity; populating a world in
which few if any things rest permanently in place.

Among their underpinnings are personal and exis-
tential cravings for atonement, redemption, restoration, forgiveness. Joseph Conrad perceived them in
Lord Jim, where he wrote: "Who among us, rich or
poor, old or young, who among us has not begged God
for a second chance."

Whether the sought-after goal is reached or the ambition is satisfied remains immaterial. As the crusty old
sheriff in the movie *No Country for Old Men* observed,
"There are some things in this life one is not equal to."
What matters is the quest once resumed bears consequences with no guarantees attached. These are the sec-

ond chances that stand for something. They are immersed in the apprehensions of life, in relation to values more personal than impersonal.

They are neither "comebacks" nor "second acts." Both, of course, have their fans and supporters. They were shortchanged and didn't get enough the first time around. They feel guilty about it. Bill Clinton played on this key when he labeled himself, "The Comeback Kid," following a strong showing in the 1992 New Hampshire Presidential Primary, after rough going in earlier stages, when his dark side became the public side, damaged goods, sweethearts, and all. However, upon his Lazarus-like resurrection, Bill was standing where he stood all along—a presidential candidate soaked in the same ideas, same songs, same taglines, convinced the primary voters wanted more of them. He was right, and they did.

Dissimilar, too, are second acts. Consider the case of actress Terri Hatcher. She achieved stardom in the 1980s as a member of the cast of *The Love Boat*. Other starring roles followed until they ended with the *Adventures of Superman* in 1997. Whereupon she went missing in action, only to return years later as one of Wisteria Lane's leading ladies in ABC's 2004 hit series *Desperate Housewives*.

On a different note but the same theme, Steve Martin, an actor, becomes a writer, and a successful one. Comedian Martin Mull turns to painting and becomes a good one. Writes Tom Chiarella in *Esquire*: "They keep right on after something new, based on what they like doing and what they can do, rather than what they once did well enough. That's the second doing and what they can do, rather than what they once did well enough. That's the second act. The past didn't make them. As it turned out, the past just limited what we knew." (*Esquire* magazine, Dec. '13, p 25)

Second chances differ in that they are about recovery—recovery of that which was. Whereas, the comeback is grounded on something new, the second chance turns on the resumption of the aforesaid, a return to the original actions and aspirations.

The sidelines are full of fans. President Barak Obama congratulated the management of the Philadelphia Eagles for giving quarterback Michael Vick a second chance to play professional football. This, after the gifted athlete, with no prior criminal record, was sentenced to serve 23 months in the steel frame of the federal prison system and fined $900,000 for operating a dog-fighting ring. Following Vick's sentencing, one columnist wrote: "The case is closed. Punishment is being administered. One glad morning, however, Michael Vick will emerge from the hell of his cell and the darkness of his soul. When that distant day comes, he deserves—if anyone ever did deserve— one of life's treasured offerings: a second chance." (Dublin, Georgia, *Courier-Herald*, Jan. 14,'18 p 4a)

The offering is plain to see. When the failed, defeated, or even the disgraced, return to the very field of their former struggles and make good, they are looked upon approvingly. Faith in human nature is magnified, perhaps faith in the observers themselves. People look with favor on the likes of the Jeffry Hendersons. After a ten year prison term, his second chance came as a dish washer in an upscale Los Angeles restaurant. He was promoted to pastry cook and then line cook. He then became a head chef in Las Vegas and hosted a show on Food Network.

James Baxter Hunt, Jr., 69th Governor of North Carolina (1977-1985) lost a bid for re-election. Years later he returned to the fray and was re-elected as the 71st Governor. In his inaugural address, he said: "The people of North Carolina have given me a great gift—a second chance." Congress, too, has come down on the side of second chances for convicted felons. In 2008 it passed Public Law 110-199, The Second Chance Act. The legislation was the first of its kind. Its aim is to support second chances for the 700,000 inmates released annually from the nation's prisons. The law authorizes federal grants to government agencies and nonprofits that provide support strategies aimed at preventing prisoners from returning to prisons, jails, and juvenile facilities. Some $62 million in grants have been awarded under this program.

Haley Reeves Barbour served as the 62nd Governor of Mississippi, (2004-2012). Upon leaving office, he granted pardons and clemency to 200 people, including full pardons to more than a dozen convicted murderers. No former Mississippi governor even approached Barbour's numbers of pardons granted. Virulent criticism poured in from all angles, in particular from families whose members were victims of some of the crimes. Said Barbour: "I believe in second chances and try to be forgiving. I am comfortable and totally at peace."

A gift from God? Some say "yes," among them Bill Clinton and Mark Sanford, former Governor of South Carolina. When both struggled for second chances following sex scandals, each confirmed belief in a God of Second Chances. Numerous books bear that title. Others point to the alleged authority of the scriptures, in particular to the biblical father who forgave the prodigal son and allowed him to return home.

For others second chance emanate out of the blue. Free of wrongdoing, scandal, or criminality; free of a hunger for atonement, forgiveness, or redemption, via accident, inadvertence, happenstance—stark fate if you will—the gift devolves upon the beneficiary. For example, somewhere in an American hospital, a critically ill patient clings to life desperately in need of blood of a given type. Somewhere in Utah a husband, mom, or teacher, rolled up a sleeve and poured the blood of life into a bank specially designed to hold it. A skilled technician makes the match, and the patient receives a second chance at life. Imaginary, yet we know it occurs with regularity.

And from the Bar this true account. A young associate, striving to make partner at a premier Macon, Georgia, law firm reaches an impasse. He finds corporate and transactional work unfulfilling, nor is he good at it. Other associates are advanced over him. Discouraged, beset with loss of confidence, he is on the verge of leaving the profession. Unforgotten was the talk he was asked to give years earlier to the Kiwanis Club of Savannah. He had taken the assignment seriously, researched the topic on population trends carefully, drafted a manuscript, and rehearsed it. The presentation went well. Among the Kiwanians that day was a partner in one of Savannah's strongest firms. He was impressed with the presentation and made a mental note: the speaker's oral skill revealed potential as a trial lawyer. When his firm needed another lawyer in its litigation section, the diligent partner began the search for the speaker. And by and by, in the associate's Macon law office the phone rang. The discouraged associate felt the flutter of elation. Life and the law were granting him a second chance.

In the realm of second chances, third parties are often essential parties to the transaction, where they inspire a vision of what an individual might achieve and become. They encourage the belief that care of persons is of greater value than their exploitation; that people can hope for respected lives.

Forgiveness of bad behavior, express or implied, is central to a clouded and complex vision. Automatic forgiveness marks the times. In December 1996, three teen-age girls were shot dead by a fellow student, Michael Carneal, at Heath High School in West Paducah, Kentucky. Before their bodies were cold, some of Carneal's schoolmates hung a sign in the place—with the approval of adminis-trators—declaring "We forgive you, Mike."

The idea has become pervasive: we should forgive those who commit evil and wrongful acts, no matter how cruel, whether the miscreant repents or not. At a church on Martha's Vineyard, following Timothy McVeigh's bombing of the federal building in Oklahoma City, with the vacationing President Clinton in attendance, the min-ister invited the congregation to look at a picture of McVeigh and forgive him, "As I have," he added.

On par with forgiveness are those who contend they deserve a second chance. If granted, do they deserve our approbation as well?

Julie Herman is the new athletic director at Rutgers University. Earlier in her career, she was the women's vol-leyball coach at Tennessee. Every member of her team at Tennessee signed a letter denouncing her for mental cru-elty. At Rutgers, however, she insisted she has learned from this experience and is uniquely qualified to create a student-care system. She maintains she has "grown as a person."

U.S. Representative Anthony Weiner, hounded out of Congress for lewd texting, announced forthwith his can-didacy for mayor of New York. Among other things, he claimed his experience helped him grow as person. He said he realized, "It's all about family."

Consider Nicholas Leeson, a derivatives broker at Barings Bank, the United Kingdom's oldest investment bank. His unauthorized trades caused huge losses of $1.4 billion in U.S. dollars, the bank's failure, and its insolvency. Leeson was arrested, prosecuted, and sent to prison. Today, he is on the professional circuit speaking to corporate audiences about risk avoidance and corporate responsibility.

Then we have Jonah Lehrer, celebrity plagiarist of the *New Yorker*. He was the guy famous for inventing Bob Dylan quotes. *The Wall Street Journal* reports Lehrer has landed a book contract relaying how his literary experiences have taught him the power of love. In fact his book is about love.

Herman et. al. may not fit precisely into the definition of second chances as first laid out. But they are close enough. Close enough to for us to ask where is the outrage? Where in god's name is the integrity?

In these cases forgiveness is not the issue. They reek of unmitigated gall.

The net effect is to encourage still others to follow suit. Asks Joe Queenan: "Why not engage the captain whose cruise ship foundered off the coast of Italy to command the entire fleet. Should we place at the head of the Securities and Exchange Commission the hedge fund manager who serves time for insider trading?"

One way or another, forgiveness is wrapped up in all of this. And forgiveness need not be confused with condoning, excusing, or forgetting people behaving badly. C.S. Lewis contends that forgiveness means looking at the sin and seeing it in all its worst light, yet assuming a posture of reconciliation to he who has done it. Undoubtedly it invites a willingness to let go of the resentment at being wronged or of acknowledging the wrong inflicted on others.

Remember the poll? Thirty-eight percent of those polled are willing to grant the second chance only half the time and then dependent on the circumstances. "The son-of-a bitch should have considered the consequences of his conduct in the first place," said one witness.

Forgiveness does not require the abandonment of justice. Nor is it the same as reconciliation. In 1985, Pope John II went into the bowels of Rome's Robiba prison to visit Mehmet Ali-Akhga, the Pope's crazed unsuccessful assassin. In doing so he did not suggest the man be pardoned, released, or that it was wrong to prosecute him.

Of course, Jesus asked God to forgive those who crucified him. But he never asked God to forgive those who crucified thousands of other innocent people. Does anyone have the moral right to forgive evil done to others?

A willingness to forgive and grant the second chance, in some mystical way, is based on acceptance of one's own dark side of sinfulness and shortcomings. Hence it becomes easier to forgive others. Ignoring the blemishes of one's existence is a risky business.

Robert Enright, a developmental psychologist and founder of the International Forgiveness Institute at the University of Wisconsin writes: "Forgiveness entails giving up the resentment to which you are entitled and offering to the person who has hurt you a friendlier attitude to which they are not entitled."

Forgiveness is a form of letting go, of allowing the past to be the past—with reservations. A body of opinion holds, however, that for some form of heinous crimes there should be no letting go of the past and no second chances. In 1998, a bill was introduced in Congress labeled the No Second Chance for Murderers, Rapists, or Child Molesters Act. It attracted 59 co-sponsors. As drawn, the bill penalized states that released individuals guilty of murder, rape, or dangerous sexual offenders involving a child under age 14. In testimony before the House Subcommittee on Crime, on September 17, 1998, Congressman Matt Salmon stated: "There are crimes so heinous that we must draw a line in the sand. We must say to criminals; if you commit one of these crimes you are finished. You don't get a second chance. The victims of these crimes do not get a second chance, why should their attackers."

The No Second Act, by the way, foundered in the subcommittee.

Drawing the greatest attention, in this media frantic age are disgraced elected officials. Here the quandary surrounding second chances reaches its apex.

A disgraced official asks, "How do I manipulate public emotions and disguise my cravings for power, attention, and adulation? How do I display my bedraggled degraded spouse and thereby gain the greatest sympathy?"

While no controlling maxim applies, neither are we precluded from asserting: For heaven's sake upgrade your conscience, if you have one; preserve your self-respect if you have any; and do something good for your district, your city, your state, the culture and the country. Few, if any, have or will absorb that advice.

So, what do voters say about officials behaving badly? Their voices vary from case to case. Nor is history much of a guide.

Former governors Eliot Spitzer of New York and Mark Sanford of South Carolina both became entangled in high-profile sex scandals. Spitzer with a pricey prostitute, Sanford with a mistress in Argentina. Spitzer was forced to resign from office. Sanford managed to finish his term. Each sought to sell the electorate on forgiveness, employing shame as a selling point. Spitzer sought election last fall as city comptroller. In the campaign, he pitched: "My wife has given me a second chance. I want to bring my vision to the people of the City of New York. I hope they are willing to continue to give me a second chance." They were not. Spitzer lost the election by a margin of 52 to 48 percent,

Returning to the fray and avowing his strong belief in the God of Second Chances, Sanford won a second chance. In the election of May 2013, he was elected to Congress from South Carolina's First Congressional District. But he enjoyed distinct advantages. As a Republican Sanford ran in an overwhelmingly Republican district, one in which he had a 20-year history with its voters. Also he refused to deny or excuse his scandalous behavior. He openly discussed it and asked for forgiveness at the hands of the voters. Where there is no admission of wrongdoing, there is no regret and no need for forgiving.

More recently, for disgraced Congressman Anthony Weiner, the lewd texter, it was not even close. When he entered the 2014 redemption shuffle with a bid for mayor of New York, one voter asked: "I don't care. Which one of us is perfect?" Turns out a lot of voters cared. Weiner came in fifth in a field of five candidates.

On the other hand, the voters of Massachusetts forgave Ted Kennedy following the tragedy at Chappaquiddick. Just as they did Congressman Barney Frank, who himself was involved in a sex scandal twenty-five years earlier. In 1989, the conservative *Washington Times* broke a story, trumpeting every juicy morsel, that Frank was employing the services of a male prostitute. The Congressman promptly gave a public confession, told the truth, and admitted his involvement with the individual. Although the house reprimanded Frank in 1990, his home district was more forgiving. He easily won re-election the following November. U.S. Senator David Vitter, a Louisiana Republican, married, and a staunch advocate of a constitutional ban on gay marriages, as well as abstinence-only sex education, developed a problem with high-class call girls. That is until Larry Flynt and the writers at *Hustler Magazine* got wind of it and investigated. When they phoned the senator's office with questions, alarm bells sounded. The next day Vitter issued a public apology for his "very serious sins." Louisiana voters were forgiving and the Senator held on to his seat.

Others with a measure of class and conscience solicit no forgiveness and seek no second chances. General Petraeus and Chuck Colson come to mind. Foremost among their numbers, however, was the protagonist in one of the supreme scandals of the twentieth century, the 1963 Profumo Affair.

John Profumo held all the credentials. Educated at Harrow School and Brasenose College, Oxford, he served with distinction as a Brigadier in World War II. After the War, he rose rapidly through the ranks of conservative politics. In 1960, he was appointed to the prestigious and important post of Secretary of State for War. Profumo was married, and through it all stayed married, to Valerie Hobson, the lovely British actress.

The scandal broke three years after his appointment. The Cold War was still hot and east-west relations were mired in intrigue, high intelligence, and danger. Profumo's undoing began when he attended a country estate weekend and met tall, leggy, good-looking, red haired Christine Keeler, age 19. She was either a dancer or a prostitute, depending on the day and the client. Profumo and Keeler began an affair. Unfortunately for Profumo, Keeler was simultaneously involved with one Yevgeny Inanov, a Soviet naval attaché who was under suspicion as a Soviet spy.

The affair was brief but long enough. Rumors floated but silence held until March 1963, when a labor MP disclosed the affair in a speech in the House of Commons. Profumo first responded by committing the unforgiveable in British politics: he lied in Commons by denying the MP's revelations. Appalled by what he had done, he then admitted the falsehood and resigned. The scandal rocked the country and precipitated the fall of Harold Macmillan's conservative government in the 1964 elections.

Disgraced and out of office, Profumo asked for no forgiveness and sought no second chance. Instead, for a high ranking politician he did what was extremely difficult. He vanished from public view. He gave no interviews, wrote no books, and was never seen on television. In service beyond self, at a rundown poor house in the East End of London, he took up aid of the poor. There he washed dishes, cleaned toilets, and visited prisons for the criminally insane—for 40 years. He also assisted with housing for the poor and worker education.

In the end, Profumo found grace in disgrace. When he died in 2006, at age 91, *The Daily Telegraph* wrote: "No one in public life ever did more to atone for his sins; no one behaved with more dignity as his name was repeatedly dragged through the mud; and few ended their lives as loved and revered by those who knew him." (Quoted by Noonan, P. "How to Find Grace After Disgrace," Wall St. J., Ju.13-14, 2013 at A13.)

Time was for American politicians when second chances in public life were hard to come by. A candidate's photo with a woman not his wife could destroy his prospects, as Senator Gary Hart learned the hard way. Nowadays, the question is not whether the second chance is possible, rather it's the most propitious means for securing one. Redemption permeates the public outlook, and discredited politicians have a unique avenue for seeking it—at the ballot box.

A number of factors appear influential. Always, the grievousness of the transgression, i.e. the magnitude of wrongdoing, is of acute consideration. Material are the costs to the public, the miscreant's family, his friends? Profumo's scandal, recall, helped topple the government. How and in what manner the transgressor reacts to his predicament is part of the mix? Whether he tells the truth promptly and forthrightly, acknowledges the full nature of his sins; shows remorse; as well as a determination to prevent similar conduct in the future;—all are contributing factors.

Irrespective of where, when, or how bestowed, those of us who have been the recipients can testify from experience: the second chance is one of this mortal life's greatest gifts.

Father's Day, 2012

rom the Athens Banner Herald, June 7, 2011;
Macon Telegraph, June 19, 2011

I can see him with clearness now — on advent of Father's
Day, clearer still. A native and lifelong resident of Pierce
County, a direct descendant of its original citizens, a sixth-
generation Georgian and beneficiary of deep roots in the
section, he was my father.

Strikingly handsome, with thick, coal-black hair, eyes as
blue as an October sky, more than one woman volunteered:
"Your father was one of the best-looking men I ever saw."

For him, life was meant to be enjoyed, and he enjoyed
it. Gregarious to a fault, a lover of people, parties, ball
games, good times, cousin Gertrude's superb piano, and
the simple joys, too—family visits, Western movies, Sunday afternoon drives, Florence's fabulous southern country
cooking, a stiff belt of bourbon. He relished them all—savored them to the marrow, until his eightieth year.

191

One could not bar affection for this lovable man, he with the irrepressible smile and the resonating laugh, as evidenced by his family, many friends and an array of townsmen—old and young, rich and poor, black and white. He reciprocated without qualification. In his eyes, all were God's children.

His abiding ambition was to live his allotted years among them, in the town, county, and state that were as ingrained in his persona as the blood of his forebears. And, first and foremost, to be liked. He achieved both ends. If he had enemies, I never knew of them.

I think of all he did for me. How in heaven's name did he? Where did he find the wherewithal? More than once, I told him I loved him, and meant it. But, did I fully thank him? Apprise him of my everlasting gratitude? These silent interrogatories emerge, from time to time and prey on the psyche.

His endowments encompassed an upbeat disposition and an even temperament. They never wavered, irrespective of circumstances, until his eighth decade. Without notice, the laugh and the smile vanished; the flow of conversation ceased. His countenance became expressionless, and one had to probe for the simplest comment. He withdrew into a silent, unknowable, inner world of which he was the sole inhabitant.

The last leg of his journey began in 1996 on a sun-splashed August afternoon, when a gray ambulance brought him home from the hospital. Home was his birthplace, eighty-two years before— the only dwelling he ever occupied, or aspired to. Awaiting him were the bed he would never exit, sitters and caregivers, and, in due course, a long procession.

And they came—relatives, dear friends, former tenants and farmhands, ministers, townsmen of every stripe—to bid him farewell. Rarely could he respond with the barest greeting.

Among the procession was his beloved nephew, a tough war-hardened veteran whose face exuded a fathomless expression, standing in frozen silence, looking upon his mother's only brother.

Others held his hand. Some wiped his brow. Still others prayed over his person and assured him he was bound for the Promised Land. He grew steadily weaker and unaware.

People called in. One, whom no one ever heard of, reported he was a classmate at Georgia Teacher's College, spring semester, 1934. Another telephoned from Sea Island, describing how my father struck him out in a country-town baseball game at Ludowici. "That was during the Depression," he said, and hung up.

Week by week, his days grew fewer. Visitors became unrecognizable, his lucidity more infrequent. Moments of inexplicable rage gripped him. He called out to his mother, dead for half a century, and fluids in the bedside tube turned from opaque, to amber, to crimson.

On the afternoon of December 6, the universe issued its summons, and my father passed back out into time, again.

At the final service in the Patterson Baptist Church, a first cousin, once removed, presented an engaging profile of his life and times, from birth to death. With this he closed: "We are grateful for having known you. We are sad to see you go."

Over the Punter's Head—Forever

From the Blackshear Times, November 21, 2007

Every year when football season hits full stride, the weather begins to cool, and the media fills with accounts of teams and coaches; of games won and lost, of the stars and the goats, it all comes flooding back-in vivid color. The mind fills with reflections of four seasons on the Patterson High School football team, the "Eagles," as they were known. And always, a single play stands forth. A long snap from center soars over the punter's head and into the glare of the overhead lights.

A single play from center at Pearson, Georgia, in 1956, in a game the Eagles easily won, on an October night that no one else recalls, it re-emerges to prey upon his psyche. Over half a century has passed. The school no longer exists. The Eagles are extinct. The players went their separate ways decades ago. Some are dead, but that play lives.

Though long ago and far away, the football still hangs there-suspended in the stadium lights.

The center would have liked a second chance, but there was no second chance. His football career would soon be over, and it had been a long haul from the 1953 season's first practice to the night of the fateful play.

That year he and sixteen of his freshman classmates went out for football. Many weighed less than 130 pounds. They were promptly labeled, "the scrubs," which they were. Their specialty was gathering up loose footballs, carting tackling dummies, and dodging the heavier varsity players.

Practices were two and a half- hour ordeals under the Georgia sun with no liquids allowed. Blocking and tackling drills consumed the first part of the practice, followed by the varsity scrimmage. The freshmen watched from the safety of the sidelines, where the scrub quickly got the message; football is a game of emotion, of physical toughness, of personal courage and determination.

As the '53 season wore on (The Eagles went 5-4 that year.), a few carefully chosen freshmen were fed into the defense during scrimmage. They refused to flinch. While playing safety, linebacker, and nose guard, and heavily outweighed, they began hitting the varsity running backs with sharp, crisp tackles. The fray became very interesting, to the delight of Coaches King, Hall, and Still.

Then the unexpected, occurred. The scrub and his teammates began tossing a football around on the sidelines. For unknown reasons, he assumed the stance of center and snapped the ball perfectly to an imaginary punter standing far to the rear. This happened more than once that fall. It was to be the only natural athletic movement nature would ever give him. Thirty years later he would read in the sports pages of the *New York Times* that the ideal frame for a center is short legs, a long torso, and long arms. The scrub was built with all three.

He was unaware his ham acting had caught a coach's eye—and for good reason. During the '53 season snaps from center had flown over the punter, dribbled back to him on the ground, or gone wide to the right or left.

For the scrub spring practice rolled around too soon in 1954. After practice one afternoon he was instructed to meet Coach Casey King in the nearby empty gym. He was standing in his socks on the basketball court holding a football under one arm. There and then began a session the scrub would never forget. He was told to assume a center stance at the court's foul line and snap the ball to Coach, who at the start was only five yards back. Then he was ten, then twenty, then fifty. Finally, he stood at the opposite end of the court. Every snap traveled the distance. The lowly scrub had found a job.

He became the long snapper on a team that would go undefeated during the regular season for three straight years. On approximately eighty-seven plays, either a punt or extra point, the scrub snapped the ball. All were on target, save the one in Pearson in 1956.

But for that mistake the scrub would have earned one of life's greatest rarities-a perfect record. Was it some kind of ominous omen? Was, it a bitter foretaste of the trouble and disappointments he would experience in the years ahead? In idle moments he would pause and ponder.

For the region championship, the '56 Eagles met Coach Frank Buckner and his hard-hitting, well-trained Blakely Bobcats and lost, 19 to 6. Played on a cold November night in Tifton, the game ended his football career. Retired, today, and with little interest in spectator sports of any kind, football included, the old scrub is proud he was once a Patterson Eagle. Yet, he knows in his soul that come October next, he will see once more the snap from center soaring over the punter's up stretched arms and into the over head glare. Must it remain there forever?

The Georgia That Was

From the Waycross Journal-Herald, September 12, 1997

Rise and Origins

The earth is old. Georgia, in the scale of geologic time, is young. Its surface was not fully exposed until the Pleistocene Epoch, beginning a million years ago and lasting for 975,000 years.

Natural forces, unwitnessed by man, altered and re-altered the pristine landscape. Oceans rose and fell, leaving a telltale chain of ancient dunes, visible even today in Wayne and other interior counties. The climate changed. Great ice sheets advanced and retreated. Streams and rivers drained the region. Erosion marked every section, including exposure of Stone Mountain as an ancient magma chamber.

In later ages, red men appeared. Their forebears crossed Bering Strait and entered the New World about

35,000 years ago. By 8,000 B.C., the first Georgians were living and building earthen mounds on the Ocmulgee River, near present-day Macon.

They disturbed little: a trail here, a mound there, encampments along streams and marshes. The native population numbered no more than a few thousand when Hernando DeSoto wandered through in 1540. His men discharged the first cannon on the continent of North America, and his chaplain conducted the first Christian baptism among compliant Indians in Ocmulgee's untainted waters.

In those days, big trees were kings. Georgia was blanketed with them. In the Coastal Plain were soft yellow pines; in the Piedmont, hard-woods. The virgin forests covered everything, except coastal marshes and grassy areas in the Okefenokee Swamp. In later centuries, timber would become one of the state's significant blessings.

It was in this "paradise with virgin beauties" that Oglethorpe and his band arrived in 1733. They were soon followed by German Protestants, English Jews, Moravians, Scotch Highlanders, and later—chained black Africans. All comers encountered a steady course of stifling heat, malaria, internal parasites, and unrelenting struggle.

Even then, however, the Georgia colonists had one distinct advantage: the extraordinary leadership of James Edward Oglethorpe. He gave ten of the best years of his life to plans and visions for a land he believed had great promise. Among his accomplishments were defeat of the

Spanish, the Savannah Town Plan, and the beginnings of public administration. He proved an indispensable figure in the critical first years.

Another key leader emerged in 1760 when the colony acquired her third and last royal governor, James Wright. During a long tenure, he demonstrated capacity and interest. His administration contributed greatly to the colony's success and growth after 1763. In 1790, for instance, Georgia claimed a population of 82,548. Ten years later, it had grown to 162,686.

Cotton and Plantations

In the 1790's, a remarkable man made a Georgia sojourn. It included a stay at Mulberry Grove Plantation near Savannah. Eli Whitney was a Connecticut Yankee, a graduate of Yale College, and a mechanical genius. While at the Plantation, he learned from local planters of the intractable problem of removing lint from green seed cotton.

Then, one day, a house cat attracted his attention. Through a picket fence the animal picked at bolls of standing cotton. When it withdrew its paw, the claws held cotton fibers. This observation stimulated a fertile mind, the end product of which was Whitney's gin.

Thus was released Georgia's first great economic tide. Cotton ended idleness, beat back the wilderness, mowed the forests, lured black men and mules and plows along the Savannah, Ocmulgee, Oconee, and the Flint rivers. It spun out the railroad and urged westward a young surveyor by the name of Abbott Hall Brisbane. He drove a stake into a strip of land that would become Peachtree Street, to mark a spot suitable for a railroad terminal. The year was 1837.

The period from the gin's invention to the Civil War was less than 70 years—the lifetime of a single man. Yet it was wholly within the longer of those periods, and mainly within the shorter, that development of the great south took place, that a salient segment of Georgia mentality was firmly fixed.

No state exceeded Georgia's antebellum prosperity. Within its borders grew the wealthiest plantation economy in history. Per capita wealth of its white residents, numbering 592,000 in 1860, was double those of New York and Pennsylvania residents. Georgia's other half million people labored in the darkness of human slavery.

Economic irony was at work in that period. It continues, up to a point, to this very day; for while Georgia had the land and cotton, New York claimed the dollars. Cotton and other Georgia products were collected in New York, and other North Atlantic ports, for exchange for European goods. Later, economists would call this an "extractive economy." It would continue to deplete the region of resources, both natural and human, with meager returns in public service, transportation, education, wealth, and the arts-indicators for measuring quality of life.

A rigid, political outlook pervaded plantation Georgia. Its distinctions were patriarchy, paternalism and deference. Powerful white men, few in number, owned and controlled large amounts of land and people, both free and enslaved. The arrangement also induced formation of the largest number of counties in any one state east of the Mississippi.

The system motivated supreme confidence. Robert Toombs, is reputed to have said, just before the Civil War, "We can lick the Yankees with corn stalks." When asked afterwards what went wrong he said, "It's very simple. The damn Yankees refused to fight with cornstalks".

Self-sufficient Georgia plantations had little interest in the services of state government. It neither wanted nor needed them. When the war came, however, Governor Joseph B. Brown and his administration seized public machinery and used it to its full dimensions. War time plants, with government direction, produced everything from musket balls to canned mutton. Industrial output would not reach war-time highs again until the turn of the century.

Reconstruction, Turmoil, and Atlanta

By May 1865, the war was over and William T. Sherman was gone. In his wake lay ashes of $100 million worth of factories, warehouses, railroad shops, and important buildings. Sherman's "sentinels" dotted the landscape and guarded a region engulfed in economic and political chaos.

The old order disappeared. Former slaves poured off the plantations in the summer and fall of 1865. They could be seen by the thousands as they clogged the railways and filled county seats. With the labor force disrupted, agricultural production sank sharply as the supervisory system broke down. Coastal plantations, in particular, never regained prewar production levels of Sea Island cotton and rice.

The confederacy's collapse wiped out fluid capital. Its currency and bonds were promptly worthless, and the entire state banking capital in 1872 amounted to little more than $2 million.

Defeat also bankrupted every Georgia railroad. In a state that had become a transportation hub, no railway was operating in 1865, except the Western and Atlantic which the federals repaired for their own use.

If economic conditions were bad, those of civic and political life were worse. Georgia government was broke; the treasury empty. Governor Joseph E. Brown was arrested. Public leaders were disfranchised. Illiterate Negroes, Radical Republicans, carpetbaggers, and the despised scalawags were elected to important offices. General John Pope arrived on the scene as Commander of the Third Military District and Director of Georgia's reconstruction. He was cordially hated.

In 1868, Rufus B. Bullock, a Radical Republican, was elected Governor of Georgia. Joining him in the Administration as Financial Advisor was Hanniball I. Kimball. All political opposition was promptly purged, and the state treasury began to resemble a bank vault without a lock.

Kimball traveled no single avenue for plunder. Instead, he utilized a diversified scheme for obtaining taxpayers' money. He was a master salesman who sold to the state an unfinished opera house for a capitol. He sold railroad cars that were never delivered. He sold state bonds for which he gave no accounting. For generations Atlanta's Kimball House, reportedly built with state funds, stood as a monument to political corruption.

The Bullock regime and its Radical legislature satisfied Congress. In 1870, Georgia was readmitted to the union. Conscientious Georgians then quietly regained control of the legislature, and Bullock ultimately fled the state to avoid impeachment.

The period from 1865 to 1870, though short in time, lasted forever in memory. It spawned a great mistrust of politicians and public institutions, as evidenced in the Constitution of 1870, one that gave state leaders a "limited trust" to govern.

Though governmental stability was restored and reconstruction formally ended, Georgia was swept for the next three decades by bitterness and venomous politics. The dark memory of the past-of the Lost Cause—inevitably identified southern welfare with the Democrats and stigmatized Republicans, Independents, and Populists as schematics and traitors.

Racial politics permeated the state, as each political contest threatened to divide white voters and throw the balance of power to the Negroes. A consensus for segregation—"separate but equal"—articulated by many public figures, including Henry W. Grady and Booker T. Washington grew in dimension with each passing year.

By the turn of the century, Negroes were made invisible in politics and economics, by deliberate, calculated, political processes of debate and decision. But by throwing the black man over the side, Georgia did not rid itself of the dead weight to lighten its poverty-racked journey. The black man descended swiftly, disappearing in the depths like an anchor. The state and the region followed.

On this Georgia of misfortune shone one bright beacon: the City of Atlanta. This burned-up town of 10,000 inhabitants in 1865 would prove the state's principal advantage over adjacent states, then and now.

The city produced a progressive, enlightened leadership. In the forefront were former Governor Joseph E. Brown, General John B. Gordon, and planter-businessman Alfred H. Colquitt, the "Bourbon Triumvirate." Theirs and the city's spokesman was Henry W. Grady. These men dreamed and worked for industrial development, capital investment from the north, growth and prosperity.

Grady was editor of the Atlanta Constitution. He wrote and spoke extensively, and he saw-clearer than anyone in his time-the south was poor; it was isolated; it was discredited, while the north was rich and at the center of the nation's life and industrial development.

Grady died in 1890. His promotional efforts, however, sparked the beginnings of Georgia's industrialization. It was mostly northern, and it invariably entailed cheap docile labor, low taxes, and minimal government interference. These offerings were unchanged for decades. The state displayed a duality about Atlanta. As early as 1882, the Augusta Chronicle asked, "Is Atlanta the state and are the people willing to submit to concentration of power in Atlanta and to monopoly of all the important offices in the hands of a few men?" A grim joke of the period was that Atlanta businessmen would gladly sell the rest of Georgia to the devil if only he would guarantee their city's prosperity.

Poverty and Retrenchment

The whole section was poverty stricken. Per capita income of the south in 1880 was 49.7 percent below the national average. In 1900, it was 49.8. As late as 1959, Georgians and southerners who lived in poverty made up 35 percent of the entire population.

By 1906, Henry W. Grady's new south politics were gone, outside Atlanta. So was the populism of Tom Watson. Indeed, the Negro was disfranchised, implacable racial hatred had replaced helpful paternalism, and Georgia lay poor and unprogressive and un-respected in national affairs. As the New Republic commented at the time, Georgia was "... in the category of communities like Haiti, communities which have to be supervised and protected by more civilized powers."

The cleavage between Georgia and her capitol city came to culmination in 1917. That year the General Assembly enacted the county-unit system. Formerly a mere custom of the Democratic Party, the state now had a law that gave voters in smaller counties a weight greater than their urban counterparts. For example, a vote cast in Hall County-using the unit method-may have twenty or thirty times the power of one cast in Fulton. The statute had an obvious effect on Georgia's public affairs for the following five decades.

By and by World War I erupted. With it came short years of prosperity, as conflict on the continent of Europe stimulated high demand for American food, fiber, and manufactured goods. Prices for cotton, for example, still Georgia's major commodity, reached 40 cents a pound in 1918.

The boom was short lived. World War I over, demand for all commodities began falling sharply in the summer of 1920. By the end of 1921, farm income nationwide had dropped 40 percent. Prices for wheat, cotton, pork, and the like plunged to levels from which they would not recover for twenty years. Hard times engulfed much of Georgia long before the Great Depression.

The passing of good cotton prices—and the music of the Charleston—was replaced by the disquieting sound of an unwanted visitor: the black-snouted boll weevil. This preposterous pest traveled from Texas through Louisiana and into Georgia's vast cotton fields. His destruction delivered a hammer blow, one that was heard in every town, in every home, no matter how rich or poor, no matter the occupation or profession. All over the state, banks were forced to close, and a harsh word, "foreclosure," gained common usage.

Nor can we overlook that marvel of the day: Georgia's network of roads. Mainly unpaved, with pot holes that broke axles of the best vehicles, impassable in wet weather—the so-called road system more closely resembled a network of second-rate cow paths.

In those years, few tourists came to Georgia. Those who bumped and jostled their way while passing through survived to tell tales of the backwardness. This poor reputation rubbed off on Georgia's proud image. It was portrayed as a state of ramshackle farm structures, tumble-down fences, quilled fields, and anemic children.

What was true of Georgia was true of much of the deep south. The Democratic candidate for President in 1932 characterized the region as "the nation's number one social and economic problem."

Georgia's civic and political life sank into a quagmire of conservatism. In the mid-1920s, the General Assembly rejected a proposed Constitutional Amendment that would have permitted a $70 million bond issue for highway construction. It also rejected a bill allowing local governments to create public libraries. Said one opponent of the library bill:

Read the Bible. It teaches you how to act.
Read the hymn-book. It contains the finest

poetry ever written. Read the Almanac. It shows you how to figure out what the weather will be. There is not another book that is necessary for anyone to read and therefore I am opposed to all libraries.

Russell and Arnall

In 1931, judged by standards of education, health, wealth, and public service, Georgia ranked fourth behind Alabama, Mississippi, and South Carolina. In the Great Depression the state claimed 2.9 million residents. Amidst discouraging prospects, perhaps because of them, voters did what they often do—given the opportunity—they reached for greatness and found it, in gubernatorial candidate Richard B. Russell, age 33.

Elected in 1931, Russell led Georgia out of its fear of state government. His administration exemplified excellence in politics and demonstrated how lack of it had hindered progress. In his Reorganization Act of 1931, Georgia's 102 commissions, agencies, and boards were reduced to a manageable eighteen. Fifty-three boards, commissions and bureaus, and 27 administrative offices were abolished. The 27 separate Boards of Trustees of each educational institution were eliminated and their power vested in a single, twelve-man Board of Regents of the University System of Georgia.

Russell used the academic community as a source of new ideas. An obscure professor, Harley L. Lutz of

Princeton, wrote a comprehensive report on Georgia's revenue system. Governor Russell seized upon this study and used it in creating the first Budget Bureau, consisting of the governor and the state auditor. This innovative measure led to the preparation of systematic state budgets. Undoubtedly, development of modern Georgia began with Russell's progressive program of thought and action.

Twelve years later, Georgia elected another fine leader. Ellis Gibbs Arnall, far ahead of his time, again showed Georgia what it could become. Elected in 1943, he brought to office a fresh vision. He left an unparalleled record of accomplishment on which was built the Georgia of the 1980s. In a single term, he abolished the poll tax, lowered the voting age to eighteen, restored accreditation to the state's university system, outlawed white-only primaries, abolished prison chain gangs, rewrote the state constitution, organized the State Merit System, got the state out of debt and transferred the governor's most abused pardoning power to a Pardons and Parole Board.

Arnall, and his Attorney General, Eugene Cook, fought and won a monumental battle through the U. S. Supreme Court to rid Georgia, and the South, of discriminatory freight rates. These "differentials" had directly barred Georgia's path to industrialization. Their elimination opened the south to business growth and the "Sunbelt Phenomenon."

Post-World War II

World War II and its aftermath generated radical gains and changes. Per capita income rose. In 1948, Georgians earned two-thirds the average income of other Americans. In 1940, 44 percent of all Georgians, 1,364,000 people, lived on farms. By 1960 the figure fell to 407,000, or 10 percent of the population. This unparalleled relocation was caused by a revolution in machinery, electricity, and capital investment in American agriculture. New tools and scientific methods radically reduced demand for labor. Thus, displaced farmers and their families moved to the towns and cities looking for work.

The 1940s and 1950s also witnessed another phenomenon: the migration of more than 204,000 blacks to Miami, Chicago, and cities in the east.

The post-World War II era saw another aspect of Georgia life that sets it apart: Atlanta's full regional domination.

The city underwent a dramatic leap forward in the 1950s. Eisenhower's bulldozers rolled through during construction of the National Interstate Highway System. This development guaranteed Atlanta the transportation hub of the south.

Mayor William B. Hartsfield was one of the first elected officials in the country to see the significance of commercial aviation. The Atlanta airport is the fruit of foresight in public administration.

In the field of race relations, Atlanta was always more advanced than any other city in the Deep South.

Mayor Ivan Allen, Jr., was the first consequential holder of elective office in the south to endorse the Civil Rights Act of 1964.

Fundamental Alterations

Two other developments sealed the complexion of modern Georgia. One was the demise of the county-unit system. The other was passage of the civil rights laws and integration of the races.

As urban populations enlarged, the county unit system, by the 1960s, more than ever, distorted state-wide voting patterns. By then, the vote of a resident of Echols County had 89 times the power of a Fulton County vote, where the population had reached 561,000.

Those opposing the unit system contended it encouraged racism, parochialism, and precluded its leaders from political life on any higher plane. Undoubtedly, it enabled smaller towns and counties, many of which were unaffected by unfamiliar change and rapid growth, to dominate state affairs. In any event, Morris Abram, a talented lawyer from Fitzgerald, Georgia, attacked the system in the landmark case of *Gray v. Sanders*. He won, and the unit system was declared illegal in 1962. Thereafter political power moved to the neighborhoods, suburbs and cities of Georgia.

The 1960s was a time of momentous events. On a frosty January morning in 1961, a tension-filled crowd gathered outside the Henry W. Grady School of Journalism on the campus of the University of Georgia. William Tate, dean of men, who once said, "Every time I see a Yankee strike a match, I flinch," courageously escorted two bright, young black people through the mob and into class.

By order of a U.S. district judge, the University of Georgia was thus integrated. Riots broke out on campus that night, and the state was again embroiled in a racial crisis.

Governor Ernest Vandiver was ready. The work of his Sibley Commission convinced this conscientious chief executive that Georgians preferred to live within the law. Order was promptly restored, and schools remained open and integrated. The governor, meanwhile, gained the gratitude of many for having governed on the right side of history.

Integration of the public schools, civil rights, and one-man-one-vote had explosive force on Georgia's public and political life. Their reverberations clanged loudly for much of the 1960s. They forever altered patterns of the past and enabled Georgia to reap the expanding potential of the "Sunbelt Phenomenon."

In Georgia's economic life, change is everywhere. A society organized around plantations, cotton, and slavery has given way to diversified agriculture, services, manufacturing, industry, and skyscrapers of "Peachtree Corridor." Where mule drawn wagons once plodded along rutted clay roads a few decades ago, four-lane highways now speed goods and travelers. Where cotton fields once dominated the landscape, now stand vibrant towns, humming factories, office parks, and restaurants full of people. Franklin D. Roosevelt asserted, "The trend of civilization is upward." All doubters should come to Georgia.